COME, I'VE BEEN WAITING FOR YOU!

A 31 Day Devotional

BARBARA J. BRIMMAGE

Cover Design by Aldous Heron

Brimmage, Barbara
Come, I've Been Waiting for You
ISBN: 978-0-9986554-0-6

Christian Life – Meditation/Devotional

CONTENTS

Thoughts on *Come, I've Been Waiting For You!*

"This devotional combines passion for Christ, compassion for others, and prophetic sensitivity. The reader will be taken to deeper depths and higher heights of intimacy with the Person, Presence, Purity, and Power of the Holy Spirit...Like Barbara, let God use you to encourage others through the encouragement He provides you."

—David A. Longobardo, Pastor, Speaker, TV Host

"This is a grace-filled devotional... Having pressed closely into the Father's heart through years of struggle, heartbreak, as well as victories, Barbara has heard His heartbeat... She's felt His emotions—This empowers her to express to the reader, whether it be a non-believer, or a maturing Christian, the magnetism of the Father's love, revealing His desire to have an intimate relationship with His creation."

—Dr. Carolyn Lee, Co-Pastor, Jubilee Worship Center, Greensboro, NC

"This is a tender, thought provoking book... Barbara has a heart for God—His people, principles, and promises. You will see this clearly reflected in these pages. Be encouraged as you see your situation from God's perspective. Let these words minister comfort, hope, and faith. You will be blessed, touched, and inspired as you read these anointed, prophetic messages."

—Bob and Sally Glenn, Saved By Grace Ministries

ACKNOWLEDGMENTS

Above all, I want to acknowledge God. Lord, You wrote Your song upon my heart... I pray that I have sung it well through this book. It is you that completed this work in me after a long season in my life. I give you all the honor and glory.

Holy Spirit, I acknowledge Your divine inspiration and collaboration in the birthing of this literary work. You breathed life into this work and worked through me, providing the thoughts, words, and discernment in this effort. I pray that it will lead to the transformation of hearts and lives.

Having acknowledged the Divine, I would like to thank a few distinguished friends who have provided encouragement and support throughout my journey of writing this devotional:

Carolyn Lee, Co-Pastor of the Jubilee Worship Center, Greensboro, NC. Dr. Lee, you have been my pastor for many years. You provided a constant and anointed voice of encouragement throughout the writing of this devotional.

Dr. David A. Longobardo, Pastor, Speaker, and TV Host. Dr. Longobardo, your powerful insight into the workings of this devotional moved my heart and encouraged me to see this effort to its completion.

Bob and Sally Glenn of Saved By Grace Ministries of Greensboro, NC. Bob and Sally, you have truly blessed my life and work for the Lord through your continual support and encouragement.

Aldous Heron, you are truly an anointed artist. You entered the Holy Place and received divine instruction on how to improve upon my original cover design. With the help of the Holy Spirit, you have created a beautiful cover design that engages the reader. Forever thankful!

Raquele T. Brimmage – Thank you for your continued love, support and encouragement. You are the "best" daughter amongst them all!

To a very special someone who does not wish to receive public acknowledgement, but thank you for your help and support. I respect that and I honor you for that. God knows who you are and will bless you accordingly.

And to others who helped to edit, sowed seeds and prayed for me, thank you.

YOUR LOVE IS LIKE A FLOOD

*Father, may Your love be like a flood
that breaks down the walls and barriers
erected because of hurt and disappointment.*

*May Your love carry away all the debris
that has clogged our hearts and disallowed
us to live, and breathe, and have our being.*

*May Your love flood our heart, bringing new
light and hope to those whose hearts have become
like the Dead Sea.*

*Refresh, renew, unearth those hidden emotions
lying beneath the surface that has swept us off our
feet many times over, and caused us to stumble and fall.*

*Let us enter into your ark of safety while Your love
washes away all spiritual defilement from our past and
bathe us in your cleansing blood, restoring us to a right
relationship with You.*

*Your love floods our soul and we are revived and restored
to a life of God-consciousness, quickened and brought
back to a place of wholeness in You.*

*Your love has been poured into our hearts through your
precious Holy Spirit. Many waters cannot quench Your love,
and for this we are grateful.*

*May you continue to flood our hearts with Your love, with
Your Light, and with Your Essence.*

—*Barbara J. Brimmage*

Author's Note

The devotionals presented in this book reflect what God has spoken to me throughout my spiritual journey with Him [for my life]. The devotionals are written from the perspective of God speaking to the reader. This is for spiritual impact only [and is not prophetic]. It is my prayer that the devotionals will speak to your heart.

COME WHO ARE THIRSTY!

*"Come who thirsts, come to the waters [to Me]...
Incline your ear and come to Me... Hear, that your
soul shall live; and I will make an everlasting
covenant with you," [says the Lord]... "Seek the
Lord while He may be found, call upon Him [for
salvation] while He is near..." (Isaiah 55: 1,3,6
ESV).*

*To the soul that thirsts, come to Him who can
satisfy. Come to Him who is waiting for you, and
your thirst will be quenched and your soul renewed...*

SECTION I

YOU MUST BE BORN AGAIN

Devotionals in this section are designed for those who have not yet confessed Jesus as their Lord and Savior—and for those who would like to rededicate their lives and renew their covenant relationship with Jesus the Christ.

These devotionals will speak to your heart and keep you encouraged and lead you into the waiting arms of a God who loves you deeply and richly. Each devotional tugs at your heart and gently leads you through an open portal to an open heaven. There you will be ushered into a new, abiding, and restorative relationship with Our Heavenly Father, through the shed blood of Jesus the Christ. Come, embark upon this spiritual journey.

DAY 1

LAMB OF GOD

*"The next day John saw Jesus coming toward him and said,
'Behold! The Lamb of God who takes away the sin of the world'"
(John 1:29 NKJV).*

Behold the *Lamb of God!* Look upon His lovely face! He is
absolute perfection! He is a lamb without blemish. He is
My sacrificial offering, My perfect gift to a lost and dying
world. Through Him, My love is manifested. He is the
propitiation [atonement] for your sins. When I look upon
you, I see *"His face and His incorruptible sacrifice."* My
wrath abounds because I hate sin—but now My wrath has
been appeased through His shed blood. He was sent from
Heaven to earth to reconcile you to Me. Through His
Blood—through His Cross—your sins, past, present and
future, can all be atoned. Look how glorious He is! See
how wonderful He is! *Receive My Lamb! Receive His
sacrifice!* To reject the *Lamb* is to reject Me and My plan of
salvation. Come, worship at His feet and humbly bow down
before Him! "At the name of Jesus every knee should bow,
of *things* in heaven, and *things* in earth, and *things* under the
earth" (Philippians 2:10 KJV).

Enter into sweet fellowship with Him and be spiritually
cleansed by His *cleansing* blood. Let Him purge you with
hyssop. "Though your sins be as scarlet, they shall be as
white as snow; though they be red like crimson, they shall
be as wool" (Isaiah 1:18 KJV). In His mercy and loving
kindness, He will transform you and deliver you from those

3

joy-robbing twins called: *guilt* and *shame*. Apply His blood to the doorpost of your heart. "O taste and see that the Lord is good" (Psalm 34:8 KJV).

Come, let Him, *My Chosen One*, create a new song in your heart—a song about His love, strength and power. Let Him take your burdens and replace them with His peace. Trade your sorrows for His peace. Let His glory be revealed in you. Let Him repair your brokenness, for He was broken for you. With urgency, come now (at this moment) and receive freely this incredible gift of a renewed life. Immediately old things will pass away, and behold, your life will become like new. In His Kingdom, everyone gets to have a new beginning when they partake of the Sacrificial Lamb. The born-again experience is a life altering experience. A seed of truth, when heard, connects with your spiritual heart and gives birth to newness of life, newness of perspective, newness of desires, and newness of direction. It is truly akin to a newborn coming out of the womb. Everything is brand spanking new (in His Kingdom).

Today Jesus wants to come to you—to your heart. Open the door of your heart and take that first dramatic step into the waiting arms of the *Lamb of God*. Time is at a standstill, just waiting for you to come into the ark of His safety. If you were the only one left on the face of this earth, Jesus would have still elected to die for you because He has counted you worthy. To ensure that your name is written down in the Lamb's Book of Life, receive Him as your Savior today (Revelation 21:27 KJV). I will turn no one away who has confessed Him as their Lord and Savior. "For of His fullness, you can receive grace upon grace" (John 1:16 NASB). So come, the triumphant Lamb of God who takes away your sins has been waiting graciously to receive you and usher you into His Eternal Kingdom. "Let everyone come who is thirsty [who is painfully conscious of his need of those things by which the soul is refreshed, supported, and strengthened]; and whoever [earnestly] desires to do it, let him come, take, appropriate, and drink the water of Life without cost" (Revelation 22:17 AMPC). You who are listening, come, for I've been waiting for you!

Father, I come to Your throne of grace where I am freed, forgiven, sanctified, and reconciled in You. You showed me Your amazing grace when the Lamb of God stood in my place, took my sins, bore my cross and died for me.

DAY 2

I HAVE COME TO SET YOU FREE

"When Judas, who had betrayed him, realized that Jesus had been condemned to die, he was filled with remorse. So he took the thirty pieces of silver back to the leading priests and the elders. 'I have sinned,' he declared, 'for I have betrayed an innocent man'"
(Matthew 27:3-4 NLT).

Like Judas, sometimes when the realization that your choices and decisions have caused irreparable damage to someone, you can be filled with feelings of unrelenting loss and regret. Though you may have tried to lessen the pain and undo the damage in your own power, you find that in most cases, you cannot. Becoming fully aware of the reality of your own sinfulness can be very disconcerting. Many of those that I have created are vexed by the sins that have ensnared them and the subsequent consequences of such sins. Many feel hopelessly bound, tormented, and afflicted. What about you? Are you freed from the sins that so easily beset you? Or, are you living a life filled with unrelenting remorse? Is there a mountain in your path named "Mt. Regret," that is hindering you from getting over, under, or around your past choices and decisions? Have you found it hard to forgive yourself, or to divorce yourself from the devastating emotions surrounding these mistakes? If the answer is yes, let it be known that this is the aim of your staunchest enemy—Satan. Satan wants you to become your own worst enemy and self-destruct from the inside-out. He has absolutely no desire to see you "set free." Your emancipation is his greatest fear!

Satan is the enemy of your soul, and he is most solidly set against you. This is why I have warned you to "be sober, be vigilant; because your adversary the devil, as a roaring lion, walketh about, seeking whom he may devour" (1 Peter 5:8 KJV).

Satan desires to devour you, and yes, he wants to "sift you like wheat" (Luke 22:31 KJV). You are in a fierce battle—and this battle begins in the mind. Just one dissenting or aberrant thought becomes the gravitational pull that subtly and insidiously draws you farther and farther away from Me and My plan of salvation. Satan wants to abort My ordained purpose and plan for your life. He wants to "steal, and to kill, and to destroy" it (John 10:10 KJV). He will do this by any means necessary—by playing on your emotions and promoting thoughts that you cannot overcome your past, or that you cannot be forgiven because of your past. Aberrant thoughts like these will rob you of your future and divine liberty. Judas was unable to forgive himself for what he thought was an unforgivable sin; and so, he took his own life and aborted his own future. Because Judas did not take every ruinous thought captive, the enemy was able to blindly lead him toward self-destruction. This is the impact that Satan has over those who do not remain sober and vigilant.

Perhaps, like Judas, you've messed up, you've blown it, and you don't know how to escape the grasp of sin's hold and consequence. You don't know how to make it right again. Face it, you have been betrayed by the enemy; but you are not defeated. I have won the victory for you! My crowning victory has won your release from the torment of sin and death. By accepting Me as your Lord and Savior, your life can be gloriously and victoriously restored. I have come to rescue and deliver you from the penalty of sin. I have borne your iniquities and guilt. I have made Myself to become your "guilt offering." I have made full atonement for all your sins (Isaiah 53:10 AMP).

Judas did not allow himself to receive My forgiveness. I would have taken his sin to the Cross, had he given Me the opportunity to do so. This does not have to be your story, for My grace is greater than your sin.

Today I have come to reconcile you to your *Heavenly Father* and *your Creator*—the One who saw your unformed substance before you had ever taken shape and knitted you together in your mother's womb. The One who created you for His glory and His glory alone (Psalm 139:13-16 AMP). I have made complete restitution for your sins and paid the ultimate price for your freedom. I have come to bring you good news—Your Heavenly Father has reconciled you to Himself through Me. You have been eternally redeemed by His authoritative and divine order. It is done! It is finished!

Today I gift you with the opportunity to be set free from the consequences of your sins and trespasses—to be set free from the bitter fruit of Satan's betrayal. If you would like to be set free from sin's torment, then approach My grace-filled Throne and accept My redemption. Accept the gift I am offering from My blood-stained and nail-driven hands.

I have been waiting for you to enter into fellowship with Me. All you have to do is to employ your free will to say the sinner's prayer. The sinner's prayer will indeed position you to be released from all your sins—past, present and future—and free you from all the heartache, torment, guilt, and shame that sin has produced within your heart.

Through the cleansing blood that I shed at Calvary, I offer you a new life, an abundant life, and a fulfilling life. If you are ready to say the sinner's prayer, then come... Bend your heart, head and knees. Profess, with a humble and contrite heart, this simple prayer:

"Father, I have sinned against You, the Living God, who created me for Your glory. I wandered away from You, who loved me the most. I want to be set free from sin's hold over me. I confess my grievous sins before You and ask You to forgive me. I ask that You wash me and cleanse me in the blood of the Lamb. Renew a right spirit within me. Set eternity in my heart and help me to live out my days loving You, serving You, and worshiping You—and only You. By faith I believe that I am forgiven for my sins and that I am now a new creation (in Christ Jesus), old things have passed away and behold eternity stands before me. I thank you Father for rescuing me from the torment of sin and affording me this occasion to begin living my life anew in You." In Jesus' name I pray, Amen.

Hallelujah! "To the praise of the glory of His grace, by which He made us accepted in the Beloved—In Him, [you] have redemption through His blood, the forgiveness of sins, according to the riches of His grace"(Ephesians 1:6-7 NKJV). Accept My invitation to come and enjoy the fruits of a resurrected life. Allow Me to show you the exceeding riches of My grace (Ephesians 2:7 KJV) and the abundance of My love. Come, I've been waiting for you...

Father, I come to You, my Deliverer, where my soul is set free. In You, I am freed from my past, freed from sin's bondage, and freed from Satan's grasp. You have resurrected my life, enabling me to "live" again in You.

DAY 3

MY DECLARATION OF LOVE FOR YOU

"God told them, 'I've NEVER quit loving you and NEVER will.' Expect love, love, and more love"
(Jeremiah 31:3 TM)!

Do you not recognize and understand how greatly you are loved by Me? Are you even aware that you have captured My heart? My heart is coupled with yours. I declare that you are My treasure! My beautiful creation! I have claimed you as My very own (Song of Solomon 7:10 NLT). My love and compassion is unfailing towards you. I love you with a perfect love (agape love). A love that is not contingent upon you loving Me. My love is not finicky or conditional. I do not withdraw My love because you disappoint Me or turn aside from Me. Whereas, you may quit loving Me, I will never quit loving you. With Me, you can expect an infinite, immeasurable and continuous flow of My love!

I loved you so much that I prepared a way for you to be reconciled to Me. I made a way to bridge the chasm between us—a way to draw you closer unto Me. I loved you so much that I sacrificed My one and only begotten Son so that you could have everlasting life (John 3:16 NLT). Would you so willingly sacrifice your one and only child for My sake?

I watched My Son (My Chosen One) leave My Presence (on a mission) and enter a sinful world in order to fulfill My plan of salvation. This is love! On your behalf, My Son, your Savior, "endured the cross [and] disregarded its shame" (Hebrews 12:2 NLT). Carrying your grievous sins upon His flesh-torn back, He began the slow, painful climb up the infamous Golgotha Hill. Beaten and bruised, He prepared Himself to make that costly exchange for your Salvation. Who else would have done this for you? Who else could love you this much? The truth is that, while you were yet a sinner, I showed My great love for you by sending Christ to die for you (Romans 5:8 NIV). Reflect upon this truth...

While you are reflecting, consider the fact that I love you so much that I have kept your very tears in a bottle. Think about it! I have memorialized every tear you have ever shed in a "special" bottle (Psalm 56:8 KJV). It is kept in a special place in Heaven. Like the woman with the alabaster box, who poured its extravagant contents upon My Son's head and wiped His feet with her tears (Luke 7:37-38 KJV). I tell you that even *her tears* have been kept in a bottle. The precious contents she poured out and the cherished tears she shed were not wasted—nor are your tears wasted. Your pillow did not absorb your tears, I was there capturing each tear. But not only this, I have also recorded those very tears in My "Book" (Psalm 56:8 KJV). In a nanosecond, I can quickly find the tear that you shed three years and 33 days ago at 3:15 in the morning. I can tell you why you were weeping and who caused you to weep. More so, if those who made you weep do not repent and ask Me for forgiveness, they will have to give an account to Me as to why they hurt you. This is how much I love you. This is how important you are to Me. If this is not enough, I have also numbered every hair on your head and cataloged this information in My "Book"(Matthew 10:30 KJV). Therefore, never think that you are not important to Me, or that you are not the "apple of My eye," (Zechariah 2:8 KJV), for inarguably, you are!

Do not get hung up on any circumstances surrounding your earthen birth. I know that many carry the scars of feeling as though they were not wanted or planned. This is a falsehood the enemy has perpetrated. Before you were conceived in your mother's womb, you were conceived in My heart and mind. You are walking upon the face of this earth for one reason. It is because I ordained it to be so. Once I send forth My word, it is done. I spoke you into existence. There is no such thing as an accidental birth (in My Heavenly Kingdom). I am perfect in all My ways. I am incapable of causing what the world might consider an accident or mistake. I am purposeful and intentional in all that I do. Whether you were born as the result of a teen pregnancy, incest, rape, or some other seemingly difficult or traumatic circumstance, it was I who ordained you to be born and not aborted. It was I who formed you in your mother's womb, breathed life into your nostrils, and commanded you to live. It was I who chose the exact time and place of your birth.

I will have love, pity, and mercy for [you who have never] obtained love, pity, or mercy. I will say to those of you who were not My people, You are My people (*Hosea 2:23 AMP*). The declaration from you that My ears long to hear is: I am your God. Even though you have committed many sins, I will still accept you into My Kingdom. Many have rejected you, but I will not. I am the God who forgives and absolves your sins through the shed blood of Jesus Christ. "If [you] freely admit that [you] have sinned and confess [your] sins, [I] will forgive [your] sins and dismiss your lawlessness and CONTINUOUSLY cleanse you from all unrighteousness" (1 John 1:9 AMP).

Ponder this, "Can anything <u>ever</u> separate [You] from Christ's love" (Romans 8:35 NLT)? The answer is an emphatic NO! You must be convinced in your heart that nothing can ever separate you from My love. I beseech you to settle this in your heart today, that "neither death nor life, neither angels nor demons, neither [your] fears for today, nor [your] worries about tomorrow—not even the powers of hell can separate [you] from [My] love. No power in the sky above or in the earth below—indeed, nothing in all creation will ever be able to separate [you] from [My] love that is revealed in My Son, Jesus the Christ" (Romans 8:38-39 NLT). Declare this truth in your heart. Declare this truth over your life.

Let Me make it abundantly clear to you, though "the mountains may depart and the hills be removed, My steadfast love [and kindness] shall not depart from you, and My <u>covenant of peace</u> shall not be removed, [for I have compassion for you]" (Isaiah 54:10 ESV). Those who accept My Son, Jesus, as their Lord and Savior, enter into a "covenant of peace" with Me. I am a God who honors My covenant. Though you may break covenant with Me, I will never break covenant with you. I know this is hard for you to understand right now—but do not lean on your own understanding. Just trust Me. Believe by faith.

My love is just as tangible as the rainbow after the rainstorm—or as the sunset or the sunrise. You can't touch either of these symbols of my love and care, but you know that it is there. My love is the same way. I implore you to accept My declaration of love today. Will you break up the fallow ground of your heart once and for all and accept this grace-filled "gift" that I am offering? It is not something that you can earn, it is given freely. Pride causes you to want to do something to earn it —but it cannot be earned—

it can only be received by the humbled heart that accepts it. I invite you to come, for there is the downpour of a fresh anointing and of amazing love waiting to be poured out upon you. There are outstretched arms just waiting for you. The invitation has been extended to come boldly before My throne of grace. Will you accept the invitation? If you say yes, then run into My everlasting arms. Come, I've been waiting to scoop you up and shower you with My love and My blessings!

Father, I come to the door of Your heart, where I open to declare my love for you. You have shown me amazing love that has moved my heart and transformed my life. Your declaration of love for me is spoken through everything that You do for me.

DAY 4

THERE IS NO OTHER GOD

*"I am the LORD, and there is none else, there is no God beside
me: I girded thee, though thou hast not known me"
(Isaiah 45:5 KJV).*

There is no other God besides Me! "I Am that I Am"
(Exodus 3:14 KJV), and I offer no explanation. There are
those who wonder where I come from?" In response, I say,
do not exercise yourself in such great matters, or in things
too high for you (Psalm 131:1 KJV). There will come a time
when all questions will be answered. For now, it must be a
matter of faith and trust. You must believe that I exist by
means of faith—nothing more, nothing less.

"I am the first, and I am the last; and beside Me there is no
God" (Isaiah 44:6 KJV). Through Me, all things were
created; without Me, nothing that you see was made (John
1:3 KJV). I am the Author, the Maker, and the Architect of
everything in Heaven and Earth. I said, Let there be, and
there was (Genesis 1:3 KJV). I even created My adversary,
Satan (Lucifer). He "was perfect in [his] ways from the day
that [he was] created, Till iniquity was found in [him]"
(Ezekiel 28:15 NKJV). Since he was thrown to earth, he has
corrupted, defiled, and deceived many inhabitants of the
earth. Many have broken My laws and separated themselves
from Me; therefore, through My Son, Jesus Christ, I have
established a new plan of salvation for all mankind. A plan,

15

for all who choose, to be reconciled unto Me.

In communion with My Son, an agreement was made for Him to become the propitiation [atonement] for your sins. He agreed to depart Heaven and enter earth's realm for the sole purpose of redeeming you unto Me. He emptied Himself of His Deity and made Himself of no reputation for you. "Being found in fashion as a man, He humbled Himself and became obedient unto death, even the death of the Cross" (Philippians 2:8 KJV). Because of this, I have "highly exalted Him and given Him a name which is above every name: That at the name of Jesus every knee should bow, of things in heaven, and things in earth, and things under the earth, and that every tongue should confess that Jesus Christ is Lord" (Philippians 2:9-11 KJV).

If you confess Him as your Lord and Savior, you will be redeemed and your sins will be forgiven. Allow me to introduce you to your Kinsman-Redeemer. He is the One who will vindicate and deliver you. It is for this reason that He suffered and died. Because He was rejected, you can depend on Him not to reject you. Having been tempted in every way, He is able to empathize with your weaknesses (Hebrews 4:15 KJV). He understands the landmine-like mistakes you've made. He understands just how much you desire to start life over and begin anew. Today He is offering you the opportunity to do just that—to start over and begin anew. To be washed in His blood, and to be completely forgiven and set free. To have your sins removed as far from you as the east is from the west (Psalm 103:12 NLT). I declare that, if you confess Him as your Lord and Savior, you will be grafted into My beloved family. This eclectic family consists of those who have been redeemed from all kinds of lifestyles, bondages, attitudes, and behaviors. At the foot of the Cross, all are beholden to My Son for their freedom, deliverance and restoration. You will be in great company. Yes, you will be set free and delivered from those *foreign gods* that kept you hopelessly bound in unrighteousness.

In comparison to those *foreign gods*, I am the God who will raise you up in truth and righteousness. I further declare that I will be your *Sanctifier* (Exodus 31:13 KJV), your *Shepherd* (Psalm 23:1 KJV), your *Refuge* and *Strength,* a present *Help* in time of trouble (Psalm 46:1 KJV), your *Healer* (Exodus 15:26 KJV), your *Provider* (Philippians 4:19 KJV), your *Righteousness* (Jeremiah 23:6 KJV), and your *Peace* (Judges 6:24 KJV). All these things I will be for you. What other god can make these kinds of declarations to you? Only I, the ONE TRUE GOD, can declare these things and have the power to bring them to pass. All other gods are unprofitable for you. Have you not tried them? How did they work for you?

Right now, you can make a change. Will you forsake all unrighteousness and confess My Son, Jesus Christ as your personal Lord and Savior? This means that you will endeavor to obey His word and live all the days of your life for Him. At times when you fail, vow not to turn away from Him—but rather, turn to Him, in repentance, and He will forgive you. Do not think that you will be perfected in a day. Your spiritual maturation will come through various trials, and the testing of your faith. But know this, He "will never leave you nor forsake you" (Hebrews 13:5 NKJV). Therefore, come take possession of His ordained manifesto for your life. I'll show you the way. Come, we've been waiting for you!

Father, I come to seek the face of the Great I AM, where I find You, the one and only God. There is no other god like You. All the other "gods," that I have sought, have failed

17

me—but You are faithful in all Your ways. I forsake all other "gods" and crown You as my King. I bow my heart in honor of You and I worship You. You shall forever reign in my heart and life.

DAY 5

DRINK FROM THE FOUNTAIN OF MY SALVATION

"In that day you will sing: I will praise you, O Lord! You were angry with me, but __not__ anymore. Now you comfort me. See, God has come to save me. I will trust in him and not be afraid. The Lord God is my strength and my song; he has given me victory. With joy you will drink deeply from the Fountain of Salvation"
(Isaiah 12:1-3 NLT).

I want to share My heart with you, for My heart is heavy and grieved. Why? Because there are multitudes that are not experiencing the joy of drinking from the fountain of My salvation (Isaiah 12:3 NLT). There is a drought in the heart of My people. My prophet Amos foretold of such a day as this that would come—A day when I would send a famine in the land. Not a famine of bread or water—but one of *hearing My Word* (Amos 8:11 KJV). Behold, that day is here! It is now!

These are treacherous times—times when you must know that I am your "only" Source. Many have become emptied vessels that have fallen into a pit of dryness and emptiness because they have not claimed Me as their only Source—and have not claimed My Word as their only Source for survival. My truth has become like dried and cracked earth.

In these times, it will be My Word that will become your saving grace. My Word is like a well. From it, you may

19

drink deeply and be eternally replenished, refreshed and restored. From it, you will be able to satisfy the drought that is causing devastation within your soul.

Do not think that all wells are the same, for they are not. If you drink from a well of inferior sources, you shall indeed thirst again. But, if you draw from the well of My salvation, you shall never thirst again. From the heavens, where I am seated, I have observed two evil things occurring: first, many have forsaken Me and are continuing to forsake Me, "the fountain of living waters," and have hewed out broken cisterns that can hold no water (Jeremiah 2:13 KJV). Then, I've watched while many have substituted My glory for that which did not profit their souls (Jeremiah 2:11 NIV). I was angry, but I am angry no more. With joy, I declare that, through My Holy Spirit, you can (yet again) draw from the well of My salvation.

Now is the set time for your salvation. I see your hesitation. Let me pose this question: what is sin? Can't sin be defined in terms of seeking to satisfy your soul's thirst in something other than the Living God? Perhaps you've tried to quench your thirst in the things of this world: the lust of the flesh, the lust of the eyes, and in other things that did not profit or satisfy. Did you discover that such efforts left you even more thirsty and proved to insidiously draw you deeper into sin? Did you find that your pursuit became like a spider web, spun for entrapment? In the wise words of Solomon, was it not all "*vanity of vanities*" (Ecclesiastes 1:2 KJV)? Those broken cisterns that held no water and caused your frequent thirst, was it not all vanity? Your thirst will continue, unless it is satisfied in Me.

Let's hear the conclusion of this whole matter: Drink from the "fountain of My salvation" and you will never thirst again. You will never want to go back to those ancient broken cisterns that displeased me and kept you from the abundant life I ordained for you.

I want you to experience the *joy* of drinking deeply from the fountain of My Salvation (Isaiah 12:3 NLT). I desire that you be "spiritually hydrated" so that you will be filled to overflow and that you will be a blessing to others who have fallen into the same "pit of dryness" that I have rescued and delivered you from. In a dry and weary land where there is no water (Psalm 63:1 NKJV), I bid you to come: "Let the one who hears say 'come!' and let the one who is thirsty come; and let the one who wishes take the free gift of the water of life" (Revelation 22:17 NIV). When you drink from the fountain of My salvation, your desert will blossom again and your barren wilderness will be no more (Isaiah 51:3 NLT).

Come, meet Me beside the well and drink from the fountain of My salvation. Come, I've been waiting for you.

Father, I come to the fountain of Your salvation, where I freely drink. I come to have my thirst satisfied. You are the only source that can satisfy my soul's thirst. And so, I come to the fountain of living water that I might drink deeply and be refreshed and replenished. Let your fountain flow in Me!

DAY 6

COME FOLLOW ME

"Then said Jesus unto his disciples; 'If any man will come after me, let him deny himself, take up his cross, and follow me'" (Matthew 16:24 KJV).

You are living in an "adulterous and sinful generation" (Mark 8:38 NKJV). Decide today who you are going to serve—Me or this world. Whether you choose Me, or the world, serve wholeheartedly. Do not straddle the proverbial fence in your effort to serve both Me and this world. If you try to, it means that you have a divided heart. If your heart is divided, I have no such use for you in My Kingdom. If you come after Me, you must do so "with all your heart and with all your soul and with all your might" (Deuteronomy 6:5 NASB).

If you decide to come after Me, I require that you forsake your life and take up your cross. You must lay down your life for Me. You must forfeit your right to live your life according to your own dictates. When you make the decision to come after Me, you have to "burn the bridges" to your old way of living, thinking, being, and doing. You must determine in your heart and mind that you will not go back to your old way of living.

I will not require of you what I did not require of my disciples Peter, James, and John. When I said to them, "follow me" (Matthew 4:19 KJV), it required that they walk away from their family and familiar surroundings and faithfully follow Me. They had to burn the bridges to their old life and trust Me to provide for them. They did not inquire where I was leading them before they followed Me, they just trusted Me and walked away from everything that was familiar to them in an effort to serve Me. Their trust allowed me to take them farther than they could imagine that they would ever go, and to become what they could never envision. Their obedience led them to a purpose-filled life that had great impact.

If you make the conscientious decision to come after Me, you must do so of your own free will. If you choose to love and serve Me with all your heart, soul, and might; it will move My heart. If you decide to lay down your life, take up your cross, and follow where I lead, it will glorify Me.

Will you come after Me? I am waiting to lead you on a journey to a purposed-filled life in Me. Come, forsake your life and follow Me. Come, I've been waiting for you.

Father, I come to follow You, wherever You lead me. I choose to lay down my life for your greater purpose. I choose to burn the bridges in life that have led me along roads and detours that lead to nowhere in life, but instead have kept me from traveling the purpose-filled "road" that You have paved for me. I am burning these bridges—for I purpose in my heart to never go back to my old way of living. I choose to follow You all the days of my life and into eternity.

DAY 7

A FAITHFUL PRIEST

"But I will raise up for myself a faithful priest who will do according to what is in My heart and in My soul; and I will build him an enduring house, and he will walk before My anointed always" (1 Samuel 2:35 NASB).

I've watched as mankind has walked away from Me and has stepped into depravity—hearts have moved away from Me, the Holy God. I've been searching for the faithful "who will do according to what is in My heart and in My soul" (1 Samuel 2:35 NASB). My search led me to raise up a Faithful Priest for Myself.

I raised up My Son, Jesus Christ, to be My Faithful Priest. He is the "High Priest—holy, innocent, undefiled, and separated from sinners, and exalted above all" (Hebrews 7:26 NASB). He was faithful unto death—He became the Sacrificial Lamb to cover your sins and reconcile you to Me. Now the Savior serves as your High Priest. He is the cornerstone for that which I am building. He is the anchor that binds it all together. I am building Him an enduring house in which to dwell for all eternity. Those who commit their hearts and lives to Him are being built up as His spiritual house—and are "growing into a holy temple [for Him]" (Ephesians 2:20-22 NASB).

I am calling the righteous to come forth and serve as faithful priests for My Kingdom sake. Are you willing to become part of My "royal priesthood?" Are you willing to

24

make the sacrifice for My Kingdom plan and purposes? Remember, "if you cling to your life, you will lose it, and if you let your life go [for My sake], you will save it" (Luke 17:33 NLT).

You must consider the requirements and costs of serving. As a faithful priest: fear (reverence) Me. Be trustworthy and morally astute. Possess spiritual wisdom and discernment. Stand aright in character, conduct, and conversation. Walk in obedience to My Will and My Way. Keep your eyes fixed upon Me. Employ spiritual ears to hear Me. Become a voice for the High Priest and testify to My Word.

The costs of serving in My "royal priesthood" are extremely high. Your heart must proclaim: "not my will, but Thine be done" (Luke 22:42 KJV). You must surrender your will and your way. You must bear your cross for My sake. You must forsake your life, and all else, to follow and serve Me, with your whole heart, mind, and strength.

Perhaps you've been walking in darkness or unbelief; or you've backslidden in your devotion to Me and your heart and life does not reflect the heart and walk required for My faithful priests. If so, you can walk away from your unrighteousness and come [return] to the throne of grace— to your High Priest (Jesus Christ) who will intercede on your behalf and sanctify you through His righteousness. Through Him you can enter My "royal priesthood" and carry out My Kingdom work faithfully and mightily.

Are you willing to come forth and serve? Come serve the High Priest who has brought [called] you "out of darkness into His marvelous light" (1 Peter 2:9 ESV). Come, answer My call to become part of My "royal priesthood" and serve Me faithfully. Come, I've been waiting for you.

25

Father, I come to serve Your Kingdom purpose, where I'll be part of Your Royal priesthood. You have raised me up in Your Truth and rebuilt my heart and life upon Your foundation—Jesus Christ, my High Priest. You have called me to be a faithful priest and servant. Lord, I have considered the costs, and I answer Your call with a resounding commitment to faithfully carry out Your Kingdom plan and purposes.

SECTION II

HEALING FOR THE BROKEN

Devotionals in this section speak to the heart that has been broken. You may be walking around dead inside—you have succumbed to hopelessness and despair as life's trials and pressures mount. When you give your life to Jesus Christ, you become a new being and you can trade your burdens and sorrows for His healing. You can begin the painful process of healing your broken heart, mind, spirit, and life. These devotionals will encourage, inspire, and comfort you.

DAY 8

WHY ARE YOU DOWNCAST O MY SOUL?

"Why art thou cast down, O my soul? and why art thou disquieted within me? hope in God: for I shall yet praise him, who is the health of my countenance, and my God"
(Psalm 43:5 KJV).

You wake up feeling the familiar dark coverlet of loneliness, discouragement. Despair envelops you like clouds that swallow up the sun on an otherwise beautiful day. Even when you throw off the covers and set your bare feet on the cold floor, this coverlet of dark emotions abides with you throughout your day. Even in the busyness of your daily routine, I have observed, *behind the lattice,* you going through the motions of life. This breach in your soul may go unnoticeable to some, but it has not gone unnoticed by Me. I see that your misery has become the size of a sinkhole and an overpowering spirit of heaviness has invaded your very being. Peace has taken flight and hope has been dashed against the jagged rocks. You are trapped in a cycle of gloom and depression. It is to you who are hemmed in and cast down that I speak.

Weary one, I do not condemn you for your feelings. Truly, "there is no condemnation for those who belong to Christ Jesus" (Romans 8:1 NLT). Instead of condemnation, I offer you My love and understanding. My love is able to reach to the highest heights and the deepest depth. You can never go so low that My love will not find you. In the body of Christ, there are multitudes who are suffering from this

28

weakened and depressive state. You are fighting the good fight of faith—but despite the fight, you have become a *miserable prisoner in chains* (Psalm 107:10 NLT). I have come to break the chains of the enemy off you. Your chains shall be broken! You shall no longer be a *miserable prisoner!* For, I have come to bring "release to the captives," and to you who are oppressed, downtrodden, bruised, crushed, and broken down by calamity (Luke 4:18 KJV). This is spiritual warfare—and I have already secured for you the victory!

One of the root causes of depression is unforgiveness. Unforgiveness is plaguing many of My suffering saints. It is a proven tactic of the enemy to manipulate this emotion in the weary. If you understood the true nature of unforgiveness and its effects, you would possess the mindset necessary for obtaining victory over this *landmine* in your spiritual life. Unforgiveness is a "dead" thing! Yes, a "dead" thing! It is akin to binding the corpse of a murder victim to the back of the murderer (as was the practice in Ancient Rome). As a result, the flesh of the one who is bound to the back of the corpse will eventually rot. Similarly, when you harbor a spirit of unforgiveness against another, it is like walking through life with the corpse of that "offender" strapped to your back. Eventually, you too will rot. Unforgiveness doesn't hurt the other person so much as it hurts you. Therefore, you do not want to harbor negative thoughts and feelings in your heart and mind towards the one who has offended you—such will only destroy you and produce bitterness of soul. It will produce the fruit of resentment, enmity, pain, despair, unpleasantness and sullenness.

Unforgiveness is just one of many underlying factors that can contribute to depression. For now, reflect on what has been revealed to you concerning unforgiveness, and start

29

removing this dead relic from your heart. Yes, go burn this relic and take the ashes outside and cast it to the wind. Determine in your heart that you will not allow unforgiveness to make you a *miserable prisoner,* chained to it any more.

You must major in the business of loving others and forgiving others. Did I not command: "love one another, as I have loved you..." (John 13:34 NIV); and, if you want your own debts forgiven, you must forgive others of theirs (Matthew 6:12 KJV).

Forgiveness improves the health of your own countenance and well-being. Let love become your center point. The more your pendulum of emotions swings away from love, the more you suffer the fruit thereof. Nothing good comes from unforgiveness. Remember, unforgiveness will only produce dead things.

Are you ready to unstrap that dead thing you've been carrying around on your back? Then come, I have been waiting for you! Come, let me help you to release it. This is your time to be freed. Come, I'm waiting to set you free.

Father, I come to You, the Healer, where I can be released from the damaged emotions that have held me captive as a miserable prisoner in chains. Your truths speak healing to my soul and break the chains of depression, unforgiveness, fear, and other ruinous emotions that are wrapped around my heart. In you, I can be set free, no longer to be a miserable prisoner in chains.

DAY 9

BROKEN VESSELS

"I am forgotten like a dead man, and out of mind; like a broken vessel am I" (Psalm 31:12 AMPC).

The word brokenness conjures up something negative in the mind. However, in My Kingdom, brokenness has a meaningful purpose. Like an eagle hunter who breaks eagles for a purpose, I allow you to be broken. In order for you to be mightily used, I must break your independent spirit. I must bring you to the place where you will trust and rely upon Me and not your own devices. At first, your brokenness may seem harsh and crushing, but in time you'll come to understand that the breaking was for a desired result. In obtaining this desired result, I have to mold, shape, and bend your will, seemingly, to the breaking point. But I know precisely how much pressure to apply to achieve surrenderance to My will. I have created you for Myself and for My purposes. My objective is to draw you nearer unto Me—to build a more solid relationship with you and to achieve oneness. It is for this purpose that I allow the breaking. You are broken, but not beyond repair. Broken vessels need a "bonding" agent to mend them back together. I am that bonding agent.

Brokenness over her sinful life led the woman with the Alabaster box to the feet of Jesus (Luke 7:37 NIV) where she bonded with My Son, Jesus Christ. "As she stood behind Him at His feet weeping, she began to wet his feet with her tears. Then she wiped them with her hair, kissed them and

31

poured perfume on them" (Luke 7:38 NIV). What a powerful depiction of a broken vessel made whole and an awesome display of divine bonding!

My Son was broken! He was broken in obedience to Me. My Chosen One became broken bread and poured out wine for your sake. In order to impact the lives of the masses, He was broken. He was broken so that, through His death, He would be the "Giver of eternal life" for all mankind. Like the five loaves of bread and the two fish, the five loaves of bread and two fish had to be broken. Why? It was for the purpose of feeding the multitudes (Luke 9:16 KJV). Likewise, your own brokenness will become nourishment for others who will be sojourning with you over your lifetime. Along the way, every crumb of your pain and suffering will be used as "healing leaves" for the healing of others (Ezekiel 47:12 NIV). Like your suffering Servant, Jesus Christ, your suffering is purposeful—it's not in vain. If you possess the right attitude, you will be used greatly in My Kingdom and I will cause you to bear much fruit. Maintaining a Kingdom mindset will help you to accept and embrace the season of brokenness that you are in. To do otherwise would be to "kick against the pricks" (Acts 26:14 KJV); and how will that benefit you?

Understand that there are seasons of suffering, and then there are seasons when that suffering subsides—and for a brief moment, you can breathe again and regain your spiritual equilibrium. Having said this, you must realize that you must assume responsibility for some of your brokenness. Some of your own choices and decisions have led to many of the difficult circumstances and consequences that you have come to face in life.

But regardless of the circumstances, I am doing a deep,

32

integral, work inside you. As the Potter, I am chiseling, shaping and molding you (the clay) for My eternal purposes and ordained assignments. Don't question what I am doing, for this would become a rabbit trail that will only lead you away from trusting Me. In due time, you will understand some things and other things you will not comprehend until you are in eternity with Me. I will exercise My executive right to defer certain answers until I deem it necessary to reveal.

Walking with Me must be a *"faith"* walk. It is a walk of ascension. When you keep your eyes upon Me, I will lead you upward and onward to higher heights of thinking, being, and doing. This transformation is similar to the metamorphosis of a butterfly. For a season, a caterpillar can only move and have its being upon the ground, but then a transformation happens, and that caterpillar struggles (without My help) to vacate his cocoon. Before he gets out of his cocoon, he dangles precariously from his perch (but I do not help). Finally, he is separated from his ground level state to soar high above what used to be his customary form of movement. Freedom came with a struggle. You were made to soar above the struggle. There will be many struggles in your lifetime—many more crises, and many more episodes of brokenness. The purpose of which is to make you a useful vessel in my Kingdom. Broken vessels are not a bad thing, in that, it gives Me the opportunity to remake you into another vessel, as it pleases Me to make (Jeremiah 18:4 KJV). For this reason, it is a good thing!

Arise, come unto Me and I will make you into a new vessel that seemeth good to Me. I will fashion and shape you into a "crystal goblet and a silver platter" for my Kingdom (2 Timothy 2:20 TM). I have use for all your broken pieces. In your lifetime, I will take you on a journey along winding

33

paths whereby My Holy Spirit will prompt you to share pieces of your testimony with those who need to hear your story about how you went from brokenness to wholeness. A piece of your testimony will bless this one, another piece will bless another. By this, you will provide spiritual nourishment for others who are broken. Every crumb of your pain will become medicinal. So come, let's be on our way. I have many places for you to go and people for you to meet. In doing so, I am confident that you will glorify My Name. Come, I am waiting for you!

Father, I come to You, the Master Potter, where the broken pieces of my life can be shaped and made useful. You have a divine purpose for the brokenness that you allow in my life— therefore, I surrender to the process, knowing that You will be faithful to walk hand in hand with me along the journey.

DAY 10

THE STORMS OF LIFE

"Then they cry to the Lord in their trouble, and He brings them out of their distresses. He hushes the storm to a calm and to a gentle whisper, so that the waves of the sea are still. Then the men are glad because of the calm, and He brings them to their desired haven" (Psalm 107:28-30 AMPC).

When you know the truth, "the truth shall make you free" (John 8:32 KJV). The enemy has deceived many into believing a nefarious lie—that lie being that they are entitled to the "good life." Those who believe this lie often wallow in self-pity and view (from their limited perspective) their glass half empty and everyone else's half full. Have you come to believe the enemy's lie too? The truth is that, in this world, all will experience trials and tribulations—the good and the evil alike.

You will experience "storms" in your life. Did I not warn you (John 16:33 KJV)? Life is not a "flat line" devoid of problems. Life is more like an *intracardiac electrogram*. Sometimes the rhythm of your life will be out of balance. You will suffer many ups and downs, highs and lows, and many erratic changes over your lifetime. There will be storms that will bring unexpected disturbances into your environment. Windstorms that will threaten the very foundation of your belief in Me. You will experience storm surges that will imperil your heart and mind with a flood of negative emotions. Storms will shipwreck your weakening faith.

If you can weather the storms of life, your faith will become like a bulwark. During life's storms, you must make sure that you are anchored deep in Me—fortify yourself with My anchoring word. If the Apostle Paul had not been grounded in Me, he would have never been able to weather the storms I allowed in his life. His testimony is chronicled in *My life instruction manual* (the Bible). Paul was a man of extraordinary faith. No bed of roses for him! Oh no! For three months he was shipwrecked on the Island of Malta; and while on this island, he was bitten by a poisonous snake (Acts 28:3, 11 KJV). He incurred many hardships: imprisoned often; whipped countless times (five different times he was whipped with 39 lashes); stoned; shipwrecked; persecuted—He faced death again and again (2 Corinthians 11:22-33 NLT). How would you have liked to walk in Paul's shoes during those times? In all this, Paul considered his glass half full, not half empty. Why? Because his faith was rooted and grounded in Me. He trusted in My character and nature.

My storm-battered child, what tumultuous storm are you experiencing in your life that I cannot speak to it and it obey? At the sound of My thunderous voice, even "the mountains quake before [Me] and the hills melt away. The earth trembles at [My] presence" (Nahum 1:5 NIV). You will not go through any storm that is beyond My ability to control. When storms come, I charge you to take shelter in Me. Focus on the One who can calm the storm, and not the storm itself. When storms come, be like a weaned child with its mother. Determine, in your heart, not to *"involve"* yourself in *"great matters"* that are just too difficult for you to understand (Psalm 131:1 NASB). Just trust Me! Be satisfied that you are in the Ark of My safety. When you become bombarded with physical, emotional, relational, financial, or any other inconceivable problem, know, that I, *the Great I Am*, am your "flood" insurance. Though your problems may come in like a flood, I shall not allow you to drown—not on My watch! When you feel like you are drowning in the depth of your problems, the key is not to struggle. Like an inexperienced swimmer, if you feel like you are drowning and you begin to struggle, you will likely sink. When your thoughts and emotions thrash you about day and night, then call out the Name of My Son, Jesus, and He will be right there. Just whisper "Jesus, Jesus, Jesus." He will hear you and He will respond to your call for help. He will come and rescue you and deliver you from your floodgate of mutinous emotions. He will set you down on steady ground and wrap His protective arms around your trembling shoulders. He will lovingly speak peace to your precarious situation. He will speak peace to your inner being—peace to your very soul. Even now, He is speaking to your heart saying: "Peace, be still." Do you hear Him?

Know this truth, when you "cry" unto Me in your trouble, I will indeed bring you out of your distress. Your distinctive "cry" has an unmistakable voice print that I can immediately recognize. It is a cry like no other. If you were in a room full of crying babies, would you not recognize your own infant's cry? I will hear you when *"you"* cry. Because I am Omnipresent, when I hear your cry, I will be there for you in a nanosecond to calm the storm and I will command the waves to be still. Put your trust in Me, for I will bring you to your desired haven. Oh that men would exalt Me and praise Me before the congregation and tell about My goodness! How I turned rivers into a wilderness on their behalf, and water springs into dry ground (Psalm 107:31-33 KJV). Oh how I wish I had some witnesses!

I implore you not to fear the storm, for I am with you! I am

37

not in the stern of the ship asleep while the stormy waters (your troubles) threaten to overtake you. In whatever situation you find yourself today, right now, in this minute, know that I will shelter you during your days of adversity. I will rebuild your foundation, should the floods erode it away through unbelief or worry. So come, take refuge in Me. Let Me hide you in the ark of My safety until the storm passes. I have already made provision for you there. What can threaten you there? Whom shall you fear there? Come, weary one, enter the ark of My safety! Enter through the door of hope. Come, I've been waiting for you!

Father, I come to You, my Tower of Strength, where I can find refuge when I encounter the fiercest storms in life. In the midst of life's storms, I do not stand alone, You are there beside me. When my emotions are stormed-tossed and problems are raining down on me, I'll seek shelter under the shadow of Your wings. When calamity comes like a whirlwind, I'll remember that You are my Refuge and my present Help in times of trouble. As I weather each storm, I will keep my eyes upon You and grasp hold of the truths within Your Word. Your written Word shall be my anchor and stability during these uncertain times.

DAY 11

FEAR NOT

"Fear thou not, for I am with thee; be not dismayed for I am thy God. I will strengthen thee; yea, I will help thee; yea, I will uphold thee with the right hand of my righteousness"
Isaiah 41:10 KJV).

Do not fear, for I am always with you! Do not be dismayed, for I am your God, and I will NEVER leave you or forsake you!

Many live in fear. Fear distracts you from understanding who I am. Fear keeps you from experiencing the security and shelter of My protective arms. Fear moves you out of a steadfast position of faith. Fear causes you to look into the eyes of the thing you are afraid of and cower in a frozen state of unbelief. Fear causes you to keep in step with the rhythm of your disempowering thoughts. Fear is a choice. To "fear not" is the panacea for all difficulties, troubling emotions, and consequences resulting from fear's destructive hold on you.

Have I not told you to be "strong and of a good courage?" (Joshua 1:9 KJV). Did I not say to "cast ALL your anxiety" upon Me (1 Peter 5:7 NIV)? Why did I tell you this? I told you this so that you would be confident and fearless in whatever situation you may find yourself, knowing that I have your back at all times and in every situation. I care about the least little thing that concerns you. This is why I said that I would perfect ALL things that concern you (Psalm 138:8 NKJV). Come, share with Me all that you are dealing with that you presume that, I, the *Almighty God*, cannot perfect.

This I speak to your heart: "Do not be anxious about ANYTHING, but in EVERYTHING by prayer and supplication WITH thanksgiving let your requests be made known to [ME]. And the peace that [I give], which surpasses all understanding, will guard your [heart] and your [mind]" (Philippians 4:6-7 ESV). Think of peace as a guardsman. Peace stands at the door of your heart and guards you from anything and everything that opposes My truth. Peace won't allow the invasion of fear or unpleasant emotions caused by unbelief to enter into the inner sanctum of your heart. Of course, this mindset can only be achieved *IF you remain IN My Son, Christ Jesus.* Never forget that My blessings are conditional—IF you do this..., then I will do that... It is contractual. You and I are in a covenant relationship. In a covenant relationship, each party must sign an agreement stating what they will do, and then each party must keep up their part of the agreement. My Son has sealed the agreement with His blood, and, if you have received Him as your Lord and Savior, you have sealed your part of the agreement with your assent in faith. This is a foundational truth.

When you are in a covenant relationship with man, you may have cause for concern—but "[I am] not like man that [I] should lie." If I say it, I will do it. If I have spoken it, I will perform it (Numbers 23:19 NKJV). Therefore, if you love Me, you can be assured of this one truth, "ALL things work together for good for those who [I] have called according to [My] purpose" (Romans 8:28 KJV). Now don't skip over what I have just spoken! All things work together for good

40

for whom? For those who are "called" according to whose purpose? MY purpose—not your purpose!

Many are ensnared by fear because they are operating outside My will and are facing the consequences of doing so. Are you? If you operate inside My will, you shall be sheltered, protected, defended and cared for. You will never have to fear.

Many are walking around broken, emotionally and spiritually crippled, because of the unrighteous fruit of unbelief. They have lost hope and have succumbed to all-consuming fears. Fears concerning the past—fears concerning the present—fears concerning the future... They go to bed with fearful thoughts and awaken to those same foreboding thoughts. Does this describe you? If so, seek within and inquire whether you have called upon your Deliverer to rescue you from this spirit of fear. By deliverer, I am speaking of My Son, Jesus the Christ. "IN" Him, you can be delivered from having a fearful, anxious, troubled heart.

If you have a fearful heart, I did not give it to you. What did I give you? I gave you a spirit NOT of fear, but of what? A spirit of "POWER, and of LOVE, and of a SOUND mind" (2 Timothy 1:7 KJV). Did I not say this in My written Word? If I said it, are you going to believe it for yourself? Or, do you believe this truth to be for someone other than you? No, it is for whosoever will to receive it.

So come before My throne of grace and allow healing for your fearful heart. Come now, and receive mercy and find grace to help you in EVERY need (Hebrews 4:16 KJV). Remember what I have promised you—I will NEVER leave you or forsake you. So come, enter into My restful peace. Enter into My protective ark of love and covenantal provision. Come, I've been waiting for you!

Lord, I come to You, the Prince of peace, where I can find rest for my weary soul, as I cast away my fears and lay down my burdens. At times, I have allowed the spirit of fear to dominate my thoughts and take up residence in my heart. I chose to focus on the circumstances surrounding me rather than calling out to You to calm the fears raging within me. Lord, I want Your promised peace to take over and evict the spirit of fear from the domain of my heart.

DAY 12

LIFTER OF MY HEAD

"But thou, O LORD, art a shield for me; my glory, and the lifter up of mine head" (Psalm 3:3 KJV).

I have led you on a long, arduous journey. Know that your action packed journey does have divine objectives. The beginning of your journey originated with Me (in Heaven). Your destination is to return to Me (in Heaven). All righteous roads will lead back to Me. "There is wonderful joy ahead, even though you must endure trials for a little while. These trials [are a test to] show that your faith is genuine. It is being tested as fire tests and purifies gold— though your faith is far more precious [to Me] than mere gold. [If] your faith remains strong [AFTER being tried by many fiery trials], it will bring you much praise and glory and honor on the day when [My Son], Jesus Christ is revealed to the whole world" (1 Peter 1:6-7 NLT). I said it will bring YOU much praise, glory and honor! So in light of your present afflictions, remain Kingdom-minded. How do you do this? By reflecting on My eternal promises. My promises are not just black ink on white paper. They are true and reliable.

Everyone who is victorious WILL eat of the manna that I have hidden away in heaven. And WILL receive a white stone with their NEW name engraved upon it. And for those who obey Me to the very end, I AM going to give you authority over all the nations. You WILL be clothed in white. And your name will NEVER be erased from the

43

Lamb's Book of Life. Yes, you WILL become pillars in My Temple and you WILL never, ever have to leave it! You WILL be citizens in My Heavenly Kingdom for all of eternity (Revelation 2:17, 26, 3:5 NLT). These are My promises and I stand by them! These truths SHALL come to pass. Focusing on these promises will encourage you as you endure every hardship and affliction. This is why I exhort you to NEVER give up. Even though it feels like your body is dying every day (and it is), your spirit is being renewed every day. Your present troubles are quite small and won't last very long. Yet, they will produce for you an immeasurable great glory that will last forever. So don't look at the troubles you see right now, rather, look forward to what you have NOT seen. For the troubles you see now will soon be over, but the joys to come will last forever (2 Corinthian 4:18 NLT).

As your journey leads back to Me, do not allow the heartaches and challenges you face along the way defeat you. Do not allow your head to hang down in discouragement, but rather, keep your focus on these divine objectives I have just described. As you traverse mountains, trek through the valleys, and go through the fire, I will work all these things out for your good. I will lift you out of the pit of despair and out of the muck and the mire. I will set your feet on solid ground and steady your feet as you go along. I will put a new song in your heart for you to sing. Many will see what I have done for you and be astounded. I will not hold back my tender mercies from you, especially when trouble surrounds you (Psalm 40:2-3,11 NLT).

When you presume that you cannot take another step, and discouragement obscures your heavenly view (indeed there will be times like this); remember that I will always be there to steady your wobbly knees, wipe your furrowed brow, and

44

strengthen you in your weakness. Know that not *every* road will be hard to climb. There will be scenic routes along the way, whereby you will experience a refreshing and a renewal. It will be during these times that you will be able to gain that second wind you'll need for the completion of your journey.

So do not be disheartened or discouraged; but when you are, personalize the following Psalm and allow these precious words to become your daily mantra. Say to yourself:

"I *WILL* lift up mine eyes unto the hills, from whence cometh my help. My help cometh from the Lord, which made heaven and earth. He will not suffer my foot to be moved; He that keepeth Me will not slumber. Behold, He that keepeth me shall neither slumber nor sleep. The Lord is my keeper, the Lord is my shade upon His right hand. The sun shall not smite me by day, nor the moon by night. The Lord shall preserve me from all evil; He shall preserve my soul. The Lord shall preserve [my] going out and [my] coming in from this time forth and even for evermore" (Psalm 121 KJV).

Those times when you feel downcast, you'll have to remind yourself who you are in Me. You'll have to declare My truth. You'll have to remember where your help comes from. So come, pick yourself up, dust yourself off, lift your head up and embrace that second wind you need, as you pursue My ordained purpose for your life. Come, take My hand and follow Me as we traverse around those arduous mountains and trek through those valleys. But look, I have already gone before you and made the crooked paths straight (Isaiah 45:2 NKJV) and the "rough places smooth" for you (Isaiah 45:2 ASV).

Come now, time is short... Before My eminent return, I have much work yet for you to do in My Kingdom. I cannot have My children going into battle with their heads hanging down, fearful and weak. Indeed, you must "endure hardship as a good soldier" (2 Timothy 2:3 KJV). But remember, the enemy has already been defeated. So come, walk in the victory I have secured for you. Come, I am waiting for you to take up arms and follow Me! Yes, come, I am waiting for you!

Father, I come to You, the Lifter of my head, where I can find strength to lift my head, steady my feet, and continue my journey in You. You provide the spiritual insight, nourishment, and strength that I need to focus on divine objectives and to carry out my divine purpose. Fortify me with the spiritual subsistence that I need to get up when I fall, and to muddle through the valleys and to traverse the mountains ahead.

DAY 13

MY LOVE NEVER FAILS

"Love never fails"

(1 Corinthians 13:8 NIV).

When I say that *"love never fails,"* I am testifying of My steadfast love for you. My love for you will never fail. Will the ordinances of the heavens ever fail? Will the celestial lights in the expanse of the heavens ever stop separating the day from the night? Never! And neither will My steadfast love ever cease from flowing from My heart to yours. When you were deep in sin, My love still flowed unhindered. More so, because of My love for you, I have taken possession of your sin. It doesn't belong to you any longer! I paid the price for it. My love is properly set upon you. Nothing can stem the tide of My love. It is fixed, established, unchanging and unfailing. If you feel that you are on the outside of the circle of My love, I bid you to rise up and come home. Come home to where you belong. Perhaps you have been wallowing in the pig's pen and you smell like the world. That's okay, your return is a sweet smelling aroma to Me.

At one time, I was very close to your heart, but you longed to experience what the world had to offer. The allure of the world drew you away from your safe haven in Me. My ways no longer pleased you. My thoughts were no longer acceptable to you. So one day you up and departed. You sought your own way, and you did not give Me another

47

thought until your unrestrained living finally broke you down and life's harsh realities began to take its toll. You tasted the forbidden things of the world, and now your eyes are open. In waking up from your stupor, you have come to realize that My Kingdom held everything you needed all the time: guidance, direction, shelter, provision, stability, love, acceptance, life, hope and truth. You have returned to your senses—My prodigal child has found the way back to Me, and for this I am overjoyed! Prodigal though you may have been, you are still My child.

Though you may still struggle with feeling unworthy, understand that I sought you and sent the Holy Spirit to draw you back to Me. I did this because I missed you and I longed to see you. Now that you have returned, I will not reject you. I will forgive you. I will love you. You see, love does not reject. Love forgives. Love beckons. Love embraces. Love restores. Love is compassionate. All of which I have for you. Come partake of My abundant grace and enduring mercy.

The world offered you many things, but there is one thing the world cannot offer—redemption. Through My Son, Jesus Christ, your sins have been pardoned—every last one of them. So, if you are hurting, broken, spiritually impoverished and you want very much to return to Me, then come to Me! Come, the door to My heart has been swung wide open for your return. The angels in heaven are rejoicing over you. I stand at the threshold, peering into the distance for your imminent return. If only you could "grasp how wide and long and high and deep" My love has always been for you (Ephesians 3:18 NIV). So great is My love for you that I have engraved you upon the palms of My hands (Isaiah 49:16 KJV) and chiseled you into My very heart. My covenant of love and peace has never been removed from you (even during the times you strayed from Me). (Isaiah 54:10 NKJV). There is nothing that can separate you from My love. My love faileth not! So come to Me where you belong. The door to My heart is open. Come, I am waiting for you!

Jesus, I come to the door of Your heart, where I open to find that Your love never fails. Your love sees me and still loves me. You demonstrated Your unfailing love at the Cross when you stood in my place, took my sins, bore my cross, and died for me. I love you, Lord.

DAY 14

LET MY WILL BE DONE

"Father, if thou be willing, remove this cup from me: nevertheless, not my will, but thine, be done"

(Luke 22:42 KJV).

I know you have heard it said many times, "My thoughts are not your thoughts, nor are your ways My ways. For as the heavens are higher than the earth, so are My ways higher than your ways and My thoughts than your thoughts" (Isaiah 55:8-9 NKJV). Would you have chosen the way of the Cross? No you wouldn't. You can barely carry the cross I have ordained for you now. I hear you murmuring and grumbling under the weight of your present cross. Sometimes you truly do act like a frustrated *toddler*. Ever tried giving a toddler something they don't want or like? How do they typically respond? Do they not whine, cry, scream, kick, stomp their feet, or throw objects at you? At times, in the heat of the moment, a child may even tell you that he "hates" you! It is a power struggle of great magnitude, isn't it? Surely you have witnessed this type of behavior once or twice.

As your Heavenly Father, sometimes you approach Me in the same manner as a toddler. Oftentimes, you too will throw a temper tantrum and decry: "I hate you," when you experience trials or suffer something (I allow) that you don't appreciate. Your tendency is to rebel against My will, even though what I am permitting is the best for you. As with little children, a power struggle ensues when trying to get you to bend to My will. So no, you would not willingly consent to being mocked, spit on, and crowned with thorns; or lay willingly on two slabs of wood while thick nails were bored through the sensitive area of your hands and feet. However, Jesus, your Redeemer, Deliverer and Savior did so for you! It was a bitter cup from which your Deliverer drank. You could not have drunk from the same bitter cup that He drank from (Matthew 20:23 KJV).

Understand, sometimes your cup will be filled to the brim with distasteful circumstances. Drink it anyway. Drink it to the very last drop. Drink it in remembrance of My Son, Jesus. Drink it in order to bring glory to My Name. Let your catch phase be: *"not my will, but thine be done!"* Allow My providential will to be done. When you do, you will find that our relationship will transcend the barriers of your flesh. If you asked Me to remove a bitter cup (of circumstances) from you, I just might consider it. I just might allow you to have it your way—but, in the process, you may have to forfeit a favorable opportunity that may not pass your way again. Why? Because, "whosoever will [try to] save his life shall lose it: and whosoever will lose his life for My sake shall find it" (Matthew 16:25 KJV). Your Savior, Jesus Christ, lost His life and gained eternal life for all who now believe in Him and serve Him. To those who crucified Him, it looked like He lost much—but did He not gain much more than He lost?

The key to surrendering to My divine will is prayer. In the Garden of Gethsemane, Jesus fell on His face and prayed, "Father, if it be possible, let this cup pass from me: nevertheless not as I will, but as thou wilt" (Matthew 26:39 KJV). In doing My will, you may have to endure your own garden of Gethsemane. You will have to prostrate yourself

51

before Me more times than you can count; but know that prayer produces victory! Your spirit will always be willing to surrender to Me, but your flesh will engage you in something akin to a dog fight. Why? Because there will always be an internal struggle between the "mind of the flesh" and your spirit (Romans 8:7 AMP).

Don't forget the big picture. Don't lose sight of spiritual truth. There is truth, and then there is spiritual truth. The truth is that your obedience affects your eternal life. Jesus Christ is coming back for a church "without spot or wrinkle" (Ephesians 5:27 NLT). Insisting upon your own way will put wrinkles in our relationship. Having the right attitude will take the wrinkles out of our relationship. When building a relationship, one must count the cost. When building anything, this principle applies (Luke 14:28 NLT). Right now, consider the cost of developing a relationship with Me. Do you want to invest in this relationship by doing My will? Or rather, do you want to withdraw from our relationship by doing your own will? The choice is yours.

Let My Kingdom come (in your life) and My "will be done on Earth as it is in Heaven" (Matthew 6:10 KJV). Resolve to acquiesce to My will in all areas of your life. In these last days, I am seeking those whose thoughts are aligned with My thoughts and whose ways are aligned with My ways. I am calling to those who are willing to go with the ebb and flow of that which I have ordained. If you are willing to submit to My will and My way, then come, for I've been waiting for you.

Father, I come to the Wall of Surrenderance, where I lay down my will and my way. I surrender to Your will and

Your way. Your thoughts and Your ways are higher than mine. You will lead me to Your intended path, purpose and plan for my life. I confess that I have suffered from Me-ism— but going forth I am going to yield to Your will and Your way.

DAY 15

YOU SAY YOU CANNOT HEAR ME

" My sheep hear My voice"
(John 10:27 NKJV).

You say you cannot hear Me, but I am forever speaking to you. Your ears are not fine-tuned to My audio frequency. You are tuned into the frequencies of the loud, raucous voices around you. You must tune out their frequency and become fixed to My frequency. Come away to a quiet place and sit down beside Me. Quiet your soul and I will speak to you. If you fix your spiritual antenna upon Me, you will increase your ability to hear Me. I will teach you to hear My voice above the amplified voices of others, for I will not compete with theirs. When I want to impart to you, I will operate on a lower frequency. Therefore, you must be disciplined to hear My whisper.

Often, I speak in a whisper. My servant Elijah looked for Me in the hurricane wind, earthquake and the fire; however, I came to him in a "gentle and quiet whisper." At times, I will speak to you in a whisper. Find time to quiet your heart. Find a place where you can come up to the mountaintop with Me and I will feed your spirit there. Come, I have things to reveal to you in our secret place. *Come, I've been waiting for you!*

Father, I come to You with an inclined ear, where I can hear

You speak to me. Tune out the voices that compete with Yours. Equip my spiritual ears to hear Your gentle and quiet whisper so that I can hear and discern that which you are speaking to my heart.

DAY 16

HEM OF HIS GARMENT

"A woman in the crowd had suffered for twelve years with constant bleeding, and she could find no cure. Coming up behind Jesus she touched the fringe of his robe. Immediately, the bleeding stopped. Who touched Me? Jesus asked. **Everyone denied it, and Peter said, "Master, this whole crowd is pressing up against you." But Jesus said, "Someone deliberately touched me, for I felt healing power go out from me." When the woman realized that she could not stay hidden, she began to tremble and fell to her knees in front of him. The whole crowd heard her explain why she had touched him and that she had been immediately healed.** [48] **"Daughter," he said to her, "your faith has made you well. Go in peace"** *(Luke 8:43-48 NLT).*

Have you ever wondered how I can hear everyone's prayer at the same time? It is a wonder, isn't it? I mean, the airwaves are congested with multiplied millions of people from all around the world who are surrounding Me *and pressing up against Me* with their particular need for answered prayer. "Just one word, or just one touch," I hear them cry in their helpless desperation. For many, their vexation comes from a place of skepticism and faithlessness. Why? They see themselves as "one of many." Because they see themselves this way, the answer to their prayers seems unobtainable. They feel as though their prayers are doing nothing more than rising up to the ceiling and filtering back down like confetti tossed in the air. They question, how can they successfully connect with Me amid the multitude? This kind of thinking can provoke feelings of desperation that can lead to audacious actions.

When you consider the story about the woman (in the crowd) with the issue of blood, I know that you, like many, desperately desire her end result.

Oh, how brave she was—this woman who endured a chronic disability for twelve desperate, agonizing, humiliating, years! It was a trial of faith. In chronic misery, she was left to her own devices and depleted resources. And on one life-altering day, after many years, her prayers were about to be answered. You see, she heard through the grapevine that a man named, "Jesus" was in the neighborhood. She heard that he was a "miracle worker." Something inside her leapt with inarticulate anticipation. She said, within herself: "I've got to go see this man who performs miracles; if He is a healer then maybe, just maybe, he can heal me." Quickly, she grabs nothing but the wind as she races out the door to go join the crowd of people who are all wanting the same thing she is wanting—a miracle— answered prayer—relief from their distress... There are so many people, a sea of people before her, but it serves as no deterrent to her. She can hardly see over or around them all. She is touching people she shouldn't be touching, trying to get to that man named "Jesus." In her ceremonially unclean state, she shouldn't even be in the crowd. She came to the point where she didn't care what the authorities did to her, this was her one and only chance to be healed and she was going for it. The result was worth the risk. Her mind is racing, everything in her is crying out: "I have to get to Him, I have to touch Him!" And, as she presses her way nearer and nearer, *through the sea of bodies*, she falls to her knees and continues pressing until....she sees the fringes of his garment. You see, she had to humble herself and get low in order to touch the hem (the tassels of his garment). Oh, she touches it! Oh, she has just touched the hem of His garment and she felt something. The moment she made contact with the fringes of His garment, she felt something happen within her own body—and at the same time, Jesus felt something happening in His own body. Yes, multitudes were pressing up against Him, but there was something different about her "touch." "Who touched Me," He asked?

Not all "touches" are the same. For example, as you shop in a crowded store, you may accidentally touch someone and others may accidentally touch you, but it doesn't mean a thing. You'll say "excuse me," and then you'll continue on your merry way. And again, someone may casually touch you from behind, mistakenly thinking that you are someone they know; once they realize they have made a mistake, they make their apologies and go on. Then there is a certain kind of touch that when you feel it you know this is a different kind of touch. You take notice of that "touch." This is the way it was between My Son, Jesus and the woman with the issue of blood. It was a far different touch then the touch of all the others pressing up against Him. It was a "touch" of great faith that moved Him.

I say to you, if you have *great faith*, then you have the power to "touch" Him like that woman with the issue of blood. Hers is a success story. A glorifying story! Multitudes are praying unto Him and pressing into Him, but when you "touch" Him (in childlike faith) as she did, He will know that it is you. In your desperation, and in your brokenness, I want you to feel free to come and "touch" the hem of His garment. Don't worry about what others might think or say. Don't worry about your uncleanness (whatever that may be for you). Don't be deterred by the *impossibility* of your situation. Just come unto Him!
Remember He is the *"Word made flesh"* (John 1:14 KJV).

Whoever touches Him can be made whole through My Word. Psalm 107:20 declares that I have already sent My Word to heal you. The Word is Jesus! You don't have to worry about pressing through the throngs of people to get your prayers answered, as was the case with the woman with the issue of blood. All you have to do is to acquire the same kind of faith that she possessed. So come, grab hold of My Word, and don't let go until you receive that which you desire. Come, I have been waiting for you *to touch the hem of His garment* so that you can be set free from your afflictions. Come, I've been waiting for you!

Lord, I come to grab hold of You, Jehovah Rapha, where I clothe myself in faith and grab hold of the tassels of Your garment so that I can be healed. By faith, I appropriate Your Word and stand on its truths—knowing that You, my Healer can set me free from all that afflicts me spiritually, emotionally, and physically. Lord, may my faith touch You in such a way that it grabs Your attention and You come to my aid with healing in Your wings.

SECTION III

GROW UNTO PERFECTION

Devotionals in this section speak to the heart of those seeking to grow spiritually. You have begun the healing process through establishing an abiding relationship with Jesus Christ. You must now trust God wholeheartedly through the transformation process. When we prune our gardens, we must tear off the dead leaves, turn the soil and whack away the weeds. Only after this painful and time consuming process of pruning can we once again see the beauty of the garden. In many instances, the beauty of our plants are not visible until the spring season—They have spent the entire winter covered and protected until just the right time to bloom into perfection. This process is similar to that which you will encounter as you grow spiritually in Him. These devotionals will encourage, motivate, and provide you with the sustenance needed to continue in your spiritual growth process.

DAY 17

ESTABLISHING A TESTIMONY

"For He established a testimony in Jacob"

(Psalm 78:5 KJV).

You are My eyewitnesses. You have seen how I have wrought victory into your life. Others now see how you are growing unto perfection through the things by which you have suffered. I depend upon *you* to testify of My praiseworthy deeds from generation to generation. To tell about all the great and mighty things I have done on your behalf. To tell about how I brought you out of darkness into healing Light and taken you from tragedy to triumph. Yes, I have performed great exploits for you. Allow these events to become stones of remembrances. Tell them to your children and your children's children so that they too will place their hope in Me. Did I not rescue and deliver you from those things that ensnared you? Did I not bring you from death to life? Did I not prove My love and faithfulness even when you were unfaithful? Even when you did not keep covenant with Me, did I not keep covenant with you?

Your testimony is My established testimony and I rejoice in hearing you tell it. Do not keep your testimony hidden in your heart, for you can overcome by the word of your testimony (Revelation 12:11 KJV). Your testimony gains more power in the telling of it. It will become a seed planted and established in the heart of others who hear your testimony, and it will mysteriously transform their lives.

Indeed, it will take on a life of its own that will greatly benefit My Kingdom. Let My good works, unconditional love, and swift forgiveness be widely proclaimed and published so that others may be encouraged and a testimony be established in their own lives. The ultimate goal is establishing a testimony for the purpose of bringing more souls into the Kingdom.

For you, the healing process has begun, and you are walking down a new path. Visible transformation is happening inside. Old attitudes and habits are falling away like lost years gone. Those old attitudes and behaviors have diminished, making room for more godly attitudes and redeeming habits. More and more, darkness has turned to light. You are submitting to the pruning process and your beauty is becoming evident for all to see. Though you are much improved, the inward work is not yet complete. There is more work to be done. So come, let's finish the work that has already begun. Come, I am waiting for you!

Lord Jesus, I come to live my life as a testimony, where my walk of faith will speak to hearts who have yet to know You or Your salvation. You have taken the many missteps in my life and used them to display Your glory and to tell Your story. You have established a testimony in me. I will go tell Your story on the mountain so that souls can be redeemed in You.

DAY 18

CONTROLLED BY MY SPIRIT

"If we live by the Holy Spirit, let us also walk by the Spirit. If by the Holy Spirit we have our life in God, let us go forward walking in line, our conduct controlled by the Spirit"

(Galatians 5:25 AMPC).

Reflect on your spiritual walk with Me. Take note of the scripture quoted above. Notice how both sentences contained in the scripture reference begin with the word "if," which clearly indicate that there are conditions to be met. You can only claim what is spoken in the verses by meeting the terms outlined. You can't walk by the Spirit, if you do not "live" by the Spirit. You can't profess to have the Spirit of Christ within you "if" there is no evidence of such. This should be a "selah" moment—a time to pause and consider where you are relationally and positionally to Me. It is a time to reexamine the validity of your confession of faith. It is a time to embrace the "gospel truth." It is a time to tear down all falsehoods about your relationship with Me. It is a time to cease twisting My word to mean what you want it to say, and to accept and do what it actually says. It is time to be wholeheartedly controlled by the Holy Spirit. These are the last days. It's time to stop straddling the fence. It's time to make a firm decision for My Kingdom. It's time to grow on unto maturity. It's time for My Church to become the Church!

Compromise has weakened the foundation of My Church, and has eroded its ability to remain the "salt and light" of the earth. *My Church* is being sabotaged by the worldliness that has invaded its heart, and the world is looking on derisively. The world is standing on the outside looking in, and what they see is hypocrisy. Amongst professing believers, there is the prevalence of fornication, divorce, addictions, jealousy, envy, materialism and a whole host of other hidden sins. These truths are leading to an "apostate" church.

If you confess Jesus as your Lord and Savior, honor Him with an upright lifestyle. Honor him by being the "salt and light" of the earth. Honor Him by producing "good" fruit for the world to see. You already know that "Every good tree bringeth forth good fruit; but a corrupt tree bringeth forth evil fruit" (Matthew 7:17 KJV). "I say then, walk by the Spirit and you will not carry out the desire of the flesh" (Galatians 5:16 HCSB).

Will you yield to the management of the Holy Spirit? Are you willing to be controlled by Him? He is your teacher and He will reveal all truth to you (John 14:26 KJV). The Holy Spirit will empower you and lead you into all righteousness. Under His management, you will find that you are no longer being conformed to this world, "with its superficial values and customs, [but rather you are being] transformed and progressively changed (as you mature spiritually) by the renewing of your mind" (Romans 12:2 AMP). As you continue to yield to Him, you will find yourself developing godly values and walking in these godly virtues. You need these attributes so that you may be able to discern and obtain what My *Will* is for your life—"which is good, acceptable and perfect in [My] plan and purpose for you" (Romans 12:2 AMP).

I want you to be filled by the Spirit and to live a Spirit-filled life. I want nothing more than for you to grow to be a spiritually healthy and productive citizen in My Kingdom. Your spiritual development has eternal merit. I selfishly want you to dwell with Me in eternity. This is the greatest desire of My heart. This is why, through the shed blood of My Son, Jesus Christ, I have remitted your sins. Through Him you have gained access to Heaven. He is the "DOOR" by which My sheep must come to Me (John 10:7 KJV). As My sheep, I exhort you to approach the portal of heaven. Leave lip service at the door and cross over the threshold into living a Spirit-filled, Spirit-controlled life. Come, I am standing at the door with outstretched arms waiting for you to enter in. Indeed, come, I am waiting for you!

Holy Spirit, I come to be filled with more of You, whereby I can live the spirit-filled life. I submit to Your control so that there will be the renewal of my mind and the transforming of my heart, enabling me to walk in Your Spirit and to fulfill Your Kingdom purpose for my life.

DAY 19

WHERE HAVE YOU COME FROM, AND
WHERE ARE YOU GOING?

"He said...where have you come from, and where are you going?" (Genesis 16:8 NKJV).

Where have you come from, and where are you going? This is the question that I posed to Sarai's maidservant, Hagar. She had taken flight—for, she was at a desolate *place* in her life and she sought a better *place*. What she found instead was a *place* of despair in the midst of the wilderness. There in the midst of her season of *running*, she had an encounter with Me that changed the direction of her life. I witnessed her desperation and came near to her: to reaffirm My love for her, speak healing to her broken heart, and show her My provision and purpose for her life. This encounter enabled her to get her spiritual bearings, cease "running," and return to that which I purposed for her.

What about you, where have you come from? Are you running? Along life's journey, perhaps you have encountered *places* that you have occupied for more than a season in life. What you soon discover is that by *living* in these *places,* you have been running from where I wanted to bring you in life.

Have you come from a place of failure, where you have *misstepped* in your walk in faith? The disciple Peter can attest to this situation. He denied My Son [Jesus Christ], and that failure ebbed away at him until My Son released him through an opportunity to move beyond that failure You see, I can use your failures to grow you spiritually and prepare you for My greater purposes for your life (John 18:15-27 and John 21:15-17 NKJV).

Have you come from a place of fear, where fear dominates your mind, holds your heart hostage, and cripples your walk in Me? My prophet Elijah understood the power of fear when he ran from Jezebel. He experienced a difficult season but overcame it when He called out to Me (1 Kings 19:1-3 NKJV). Like Elijah, I can move you beyond your fear and give you the faith and strength to confront any circumstance that you face in life, If you call out to Me, stand in My truth, recall My promises, and reflect upon My faithfulness in your life.

Have you come from a place of disillusionment, where what you expected in your walk in Me proved instead to be a detour characterized by fiery trials, challenges, and life storms that seem too hard to bear and weather? Job wrestled with this painful emotion as his faith was severely tested. My ears were inclined to hear his cries to Me as I taught him to trust me to bring him through his prolong season of testing (Job 10:1-22 ESV). I will bring you through any season in the valley, desert, or wilderness in life, if you will call out to Me and trust Me to walk beside you through times of difficulty.

Have you come from a place of rebellion, where you have run from My call and purpose in your life? You have heard My call to you, but you closed your ears, hardened your heart, and tried to run as far away as you could, in an attempt to escape from My purpose—yet your efforts failed.

67

This is what My rebellious prophet, Jonah learned. He ran from My call to preach to the people in Nineveh, but he could not outrun Me. After being swallowed by a whale, he learned that He could not run away from My ordained purpose in His life (Jonah 1 & 2 ESV). Neither can you continue to run away in rebellion and not face the consequences. Obedience is the only answer to My call to you.

Where are you going? Are you going to continue to run deeper into those *places* which have a stronghold over you, or will you run to Me? If you return to Me, together we can revisit those *places* that you ran from and evict their power over your heart and life. It requires that you reset your spiritual compass upon Me, where you will find your way to My will, plan, purpose, healing and direction. If you would forsake those places you've lived in, and follow My way, I will lead you along the road to My best in life.

Are you weary from your running? If so, come find rest in Me. Come, I've been waiting for you.

Father, I come seeking rest for my weary soul and tired feet. I want to stop running. Replenish and strengthen my soul so that I can confront that which I have been running from, and prepare my feet to walk to those places where You have purposed for me in life.

DAY 20

WILL YOU BE THE ONE?

"Therefore, we are ambassadors for Christ, certain that God is appealing through us. We plead on Christ's behalf, "Be reconciled to God" (2 Corinthians 5:20 HCSB).

Do not be deceived, there is a great falling away happening right before your very eyes. Do you not perceive it? Many of My children no longer identify with Me. The landscape of My church is changing. The bride of Christ is not ready for My coming. You must get ready to meet the Bridegroom! Time is short and getting shorter. There are many (in the world) who still do not have a relationship with My Son. They know of Him, but they have not accepted Him as their Lord and Savior. They do not believe they need a Savior. They have chosen to live their lives for themselves. They love and cherish the world and everything that the world has to offer (1 John 2:15 KJV). Their confidence is in their own abilities and resources. These are the *unreached!*

Though the unreached are not *reaching* out to Me, I am still *reaching* out to them. There is a great need for My church to step up to their responsibility and focus on that which is important to the Kingdom. I need Ambassadors for Christ to go forth into their communities, nations, and the world sharing the good news of Salvation. This is your mandate. This is what you are called to do. I am calling you to humble yourself and think about someone other than yourself. I am placing a conviction upon your heart to lead the unreached to Me, and the backslider back to Me. I am

69

calling you to help them to grow and mature in their faith. I am calling you to help steady their walk in Me. I call you out to make a difference in the world (for My sake). This world is passing away and sobriety is the buzzword for the day! Do not be lulled to sleep by focusing on one's own achievements and one's own gratification. Do not be caught up in the world and go down with the ship. "For what shall it profit a man, if he shall gain [all that the world has to offer], and lose his own soul (Mark 8:36 KJV)?"

Faithful one, I want to know:

Who'll be an Ambassador for Christ?
Who'll proclaim His word abroad for Him?
Who'll sacrifice their life for His cause?
Who'll be an ambassador for Christ?

Will you be the one He's looking for?
Will you proclaim His word abroad for Him?
Will you sacrifice your life for His cause?
Will you be an Ambassador for Christ?

Faithful one, I want to know: will you be the one? If you'll say, "I'll go," then come, for I've been waiting for you!

Lord, I come to be a voice for You, whereby I will lay down my life to fulfill Your call to touch hearts and lives for Your Kingdom sake. Strengthen my faith, equip me with courage, and prepare my feet to go out and proclaim the Gospel to lost souls everywhere You lead me.

DAY 21

BE YE HOLY

"Because it is written, be ye holy; for I am holy"
(1 Peter 1:16 KJV).

There is a shifting going on in the world around you. Like a giant boulder that is threatening to crash and crush everything in its path, so is the world teetering on the edge of disaster. All humanity senses the change. Everything is changing. There is a diabolical campaign to shift away from My statutes and precepts. Everything that My Word stands for (globally) is under attack. Morals are changing. What is *right* is now deemed *wrong*—and what is *wrong* is perceived *right*. Idolatry is rampant. Where is the Church in the midst of all this shifting? Where are *you*? Where do *you* stand in the face of all that is happening around you? Are you standing up for My Son, Jesus Christ? Are you standing your ground for righteousness sake? Or, are you compromising your beliefs due to fear of being persecuted or ostracized? Are you reluctant to stand out in the crowd so that you can "hide" your faith in Me? Where do you stand? Are you "employing your freedom as a pretext for wickedness" (1 Peter 2:16 AMPC)? Or, are you standing firm for Kingdom sake?

Now is not the time to compromise or abandon My timeless truths. My "Word is true from the beginning; and every one of My righteous judgments endureth forever" (Psalm 119:160 KJV). My truths will never change. My truths do not adapt to world's views, philosophy, or persuasion. My truths trump the truths of the world. In My Word, you will find

71

My perspective on everything that you are experiencing in this world. The world will be judged according to the precepts in My written Word. "He who rejects Me, and does NOT receive My Words, has that which judges him—the Word that I have spoken will judge him in the last day" (John 12:48 NKJV).

I challenge you to not go with the *flow!* Do not follow after unrighteousness. Do not shift away from My sound doctrine. Though the majority of the world may compromise their morals and values and attempt to legislate sin according to what the world dictates, let not the Church depart from My Truth. The Word tells you to "be holy, for I am holy" (1 Peter 1:16 NKJV). You must be like the first church. They were persecuted for righteousness' sake. Though they were persecuted, the church grew and became strong. Now is not the time to be lukewarm or slack. Stand your ground! Stay strong! Did you mean it when you proclaimed: "as for me and my household, we will serve the Lord" (Joshua 24:15 NIV)?

I have made it abundantly clear, "that in the last days perilous times will come" (2 Timothy 3:1 NKJV). I did not say that perilous times may come, or might come. I foretold of the time when men would be lovers of themselves, covetous, boasters, proud, blasphemers, disobedient to parents, unthankful and UNHOLY, did I not?

You are currently living in these prophesied times. So why are you surprised that people no longer have natural affection for Me, or for one another? You are witnesses to the fact that the world is full of compromisers, trucebreakers, and false accusers. You stand as witnesses that they are despisers of that which is good and those seeking to do good [to walk in Me]. In these last days, people will be "traitors, headstrong, haughty, lovers of pleasure rather than lovers of [ME]." Truly there exist a form of godliness (that surrounds you), but My power has been denied (2 Timothy 3:2-5 NKJV).

Therefore, faithful one, in these perilous times, you have the opportunity to shine for the Kingdom. "As a stranger and a pilgrim, let your conversation be honest amongst the unbelievers. "Whereas they speak against you, as evildoers, they may, by your good works, which they SHALL behold, glorify [Me] in the day of visitation" (1 Peter 2:11-12 KJV). Do not allow your heart and mind to be swayed by popular opinion or contaminated by the shifting truths of the moment. No, your mandate is to continue "perfecting holiness out of reverence for [Me]" (2 Corinthians 7:1 NIV).

Are you willing to be set apart for My Kingdom purposes? Are you willing to destroy "every lofty thing raised up" against My wisdom, ways, and truth (2 Corinthians 10:5 NASB)? Are you willing to take up your cross and continue following Me despite all that you see, hear, and experience? If your answer is yes, then come, for I've been waiting for you! Come on through the open door and into My waiting arms. You are on "MY" team!

Father, I come to the altar of Your heart, where I commit to stand on holy ground, take up my cross, and walk in holiness. I forsake the world's ways and philosophies—I want to be set apart for You and Your Kingdom purposes. I purpose in my heart to get rooted, grounded, and settled in you, so that when the rains and floods come, and the winds blow, I will be found standing on Your Word and standing up for holiness sake.

DAY 22

PUT ME FIRST

"But FIRST make a small loaf of bread for me from what you have and bring it to me, and THEN make something for yourself and your son" (1 Kings 17:13 NIV).

Imagine that you are going through a difficult time and all your resources have run as dry as a sapless tree. The refrigerator is empty and the cupboards are bare except for a handful of flour in a non-descript container and a spoonful of cooking oil in a small jar. That's all you have left to survive on. Furthermore, from this, you have to feed yourself and your child. With a heavy heart, you reach for the meager ingredients to prepare what is perhaps your last meal. But before you can open up the cupboard, you hear a knock at the door. You open up the door and there stands a stranger on the other side of the threshold asking for a drink of water. As you turn to accommodate him, he calmly announces that he would also like something to eat. What would be your reaction? Would you accommodate the stranger at the door? Would you put him first above your own needs? Would you give him a portion of your child's last meal? Would you trust him when he says that God will provide a miracle for you if you would share from your lack? For the widowed woman that Elijah approached, the promise to provide was conditional. IF she followed the stranger's instruction, THEN she would have ample provision for the present and the future. "Elijah said to her, Fear not; go and do as you have said. But make me a little cake of it <u>first</u> and bring it to me, and <u>afterward</u> prepare some for yourself and your son. For thus says the Lord, the God of Israel: The jar of meal shall not waste away or the bottle of oil fail until the day that the Lord sends rain on the earth" (1 Kings 17:13-14 AMPC). I cannot emphasize enough the importance of adhering to the conditions required for receiving My provision and My blessings.

What is your need today? Are you willing to put Me first in order to receive what you're seeking? If you put Me first, above all, then you will be abundantly blessed. You would have ample provision for the present and the future by sharing from your lack. You ponder this, and you don't see how. You just don't see how you can carve out any more time out of your busy life because you're already overwhelmed. Like the widowed woman, just trust Me. You'll find that your time will be divinely stretched when you put Me first and you purpose to spend more time fellowshipping with Me. Through supernatural means, you will be able to do more than you ever thought possible.

Now it's time for introspection. Has it been very challenging for you to give Me the first portion of your life—the choice portion of your day? Is it difficult for you to take the time to accommodate Me? As you go about your day, is it too much to ask that you put Me first, above all, and spend time with Me? I stand at the door of your heart waiting to be invited in to share your life with you. Reflect on all the things that compete for your time with Me? Think of all the activities done under the sun that distract you away from making Me your priority. At times, the Kingdom work that you labor to do on My behalf can prevent you from spending quality time with Me. How long has it been since you have spent memorable time with Me? How many minutes out of the day? How many hours out of the week? When you had the choice of spending time with Me or enjoying some pleasant activity, which did you choose? The world is crowding Me out of their lives. Are you? I am jealous of those things that you put before Me. I created you for companionship. I long to fellowship with you. I created you for My pleasure and My glory!

Come set apart some time just for Me. Let us fellowship with one another. You share your heart with Me, and I'll share My heart with you. Take the time to show Me love, affection and adoration. Make Me feel like I am a significant part of your life. Decide if our relationship is as important to you as it is to Me. Come back to your first love—come back to Me. Put Me first, above all. Come, I've been waiting for you!

Lord, I come to crown You king, where you will reign within my heart and over my life. I will put You first above all. I will give You the choice portion of my life. I will die to myself so that I can live for You.

DAY 23

SEEK MY COUNSEL

"The counsel of the Lord stands forever.
The plans of His heart from generation to generation"
(Psalm 33:11 NASB).

As I sit on My heavenly throne, I have a panoramic view of the world and all of its citizens. Regardless of what part of the world you hail from, there are countless others, just like you, who ponder and make difficult choices and decisions each day. I know every decision you have made in your lifetime. They are beyond your capability to calculate. Do you find it amazing that, in My possession, I hold an accurate record of every decision you have made over the course of your life and the outcome of each decision? I know this because I am omniscient—all-knowing, all-wise, and all-seeing.

I've watched every decision you made in life. Some were good and some were bad. Some decisions have had disastrous consequences and have brought you great sorrow. Some decisions have led to blessings, and have brought you great joy. Some decisions have been life altering.

Even when you employ your best knowledge, insight, intellect, capability, and effort, you still do not possess the capacity to make sound decisions all the time. Why? Because you are not all-knowing, all-wise, or all-seeing? This is why you must not "lean on your own understanding." You must constantly seek My divine

77

wisdom and counsel. On a scale of one to ten, how would you rate your ability to make good decisions? Would you like to improve the quality of your decision making? If you would, it is possible.

Where to start? You must first seek My counsel. Begin this process by turning to My written Word (the Bible) for discernment. My counsel is reflected in every word and on every page. In Psalm 32:8, I have asserted that "I will instruct you and teach you in the way which you should go; I will counsel you with My eye upon you" (NASB). As you grow spiritually, I will reveal to you deeper truths that go beyond the surface of My Word. When you seek My divine counsel, I will provide you with divine direction, revelation, and impartation. I will guide you and point you to crucial *markers* along the way.

What is a *guide* and when is a *guide* needed? A *guide* is one who has more skill and knowledge. He is one who has gone ahead and mapped out the terrain and the lay of the land, just like a shepherd. When is a *guide* needed? A *guide* is needed when one does not know the way—like sheep. Sheep must have a shepherd to guide them. They need the shepherd to go before them and map out the terrain and watering holes.

My precious sheep, you were not meant to go it alone in this world. You need a *guide*. You need a shepherd that will lead you in life. That Shepherd is My Son, Jesus Christ. He has gone before you, and now he has come back to lead you to My desired haven. I have a plan for you and I desire to lead you according to My plan for your life. This is why you must seek My counsel at all times. You cannot run ahead of Me, or you will make wrong turns and wrong decisions in life. Make it a practice of seeking Me. Ask Me, "is this the way that I should go?" Ask Me, "is this the way that leads to Your path for me?" Ask Me, "does my plan align with Your will for me?" Ask Me, "Father, is this what is best for me?" Working in this way, you are seeking My counsel. Walking in this way, you can avoid many pitfalls and landmines. Staying in this way, you will not wander off course. In this way, you can begin to live in My perfect will for your life.

The key to making better choices for your life, and the lives of those you impact, is to remain in constant communion with Me. Is there a situation that you need to resolve in your life today? Is there some problem that you are incapable of solving? Do you find yourself at a fork in the road, lost, and do not know which way you should go? Then come, let the counsel of My Word shine a light on your path. Come and get insight, discernment, and direction. Come, I will show you the way. Come, I've been waiting for you!

Lord, I come to seek Your counsel, where You will be my Guide and I will follow where You lead. At times, I sought those that could not lead me or guide me in the set path that You had for me—I went to Egypt and Assyria—which lead to costly mistakes along the way. I've learned that nothing compares to the guidance and wisdom that You impart. Open up my spiritual ears to hear, and my spiritual heart to receive Your divine instruction for my life.

DAY 24

LEAVE THE PAST BEHIND

"I do not consider, brethren, that I have captured and made it my own [yet]; but one thing I do [it is my own aspiration]: forgetting what lies behind and straining forward to what lies ahead. I press on toward the goal to win [the supreme and heavenly] prize to which God in Christ Jesus is calling us upward"
(Philippians 3:13-14 AMPC).

Do you want everything that I have ordained for you? Do you know how to position yourself to obtain it? How badly do you want what I have purposed for you? Do you want it bad enough to let go of the past? Bad enough to forgive yourself for the unforgiveable things you think you've done? Bad enough to stop punishing yourself for everything you've done wrong in life? Bad enough to forgive those that have wronged and wounded you? Bad enough to say to those who have hurt you: "I'm standing in God, I'm standing in forgiveness. You 'thought evil against me, but God meant it unto good,' to bring to pass those things He has ordained for my life" (Genesis 50:20 KJV).

You must resolve to break with the past in order to embrace the new. You must reposition yourself, *NOW*, to make room for the *NEW!* Your old life is gone—your new life is burgeoning (2 Corinthian 5:17 TM).

Is unforgiveness residing in your heart and keeping you in bondage? Is unforgiveness towards others or for yourself, holding you hostage to the past? Remember, I said; "If

80

[you] confess your sins, [I will be] faithful and just and will forgive [you] for your sins and purify [you] from all unrighteousness" (1 John 1:9 NIV). If I have forgiven you for your sins, shouldn't you be about the business of forgiving yourself and forgiving others who have sinned against you? Furthermore, I have said that "If you forgive others for their transgressions, [I, Your] heavenly Father will also forgive you. But if you do not forgive others, then [I] will not forgive your transgressions" (Matthew 6:14-15 NASB).

Right now, I want you to do some soul searching. Reflect on all who have wronged and wounded you in life (including yourself). Resolve to forgive them (yourself) and remit unforgiveness from your heart, and I will remit their (your) offense from My mind and will remember no more.

Today can be your day of emancipation. You must make a conscientious decision to leave the past behind. You have a choice to make. You can hang on to the past, or you can let it go. If you let it go, "here's what I'm going to do...: I'll pour pure water over you and scrub you clean. I'll give you a new heart [and will] put a new spirit in you. I'll remove the stone heart from your body and replace it with a heart that's God-willed, not self-willed. I'll put My Spirit in you and make it possible for you to do what I tell you to do, and live by My commands...[You'll be my mine and] I'll be your God" (Ezekiel 36:26-28 TM). You'll be My witness upon the earth. I know what I am asking you is not easy to do. For you may be womb-wounded. You may have experienced emotional trauma in the womb. You may have experienced rejection in the womb. Whatever the case may be, My child, you must labor to forget and strain forward to receive the new thing I'm doing in your heart and life. Focus on the goal. The goal is to perceive and understand what My will is for your life and begin to walk in it and become who you are in Christ Jesus. Become that new creation! To do so, you have to strain for it. You have to reach higher and higher and higher until you grab hold of it. When you obtain it, your victory will be sweet! Oh yes, what the devil meant for evil has become the necessary ingredients that have made you into who you are today—a strong soldier in My Kingdom—fit for My use. You see, your enemy does not want you to be victorious. He wants you weak and distracted by things from the past, and not fit for the Kingdom or anything else. When you stand firm in Me, with hands on your hips, and proclaim to your nemesis: "Enough!" You will not control me any longer by having me living in the past, harboring painful emotions, wallowing in self-pity and forfeiting my future," the enemy will run. Let your new mantra become: "Onward Christian soldier." When you do this, look out, for you will become formidable in the eyes of the enemy. Yes, you will make him stop in his tracks and flee from you for a change. Isn't this what you want? Don't you want to be more than a conqueror? Don't you want to capture what the future holds and make it your own? Don't you want to forget what is lying behind you? Don't you want to strain forward to what lies ahead? Are you ready to press on towards the goal? Are you ready to win that heavenly prize to which Christ Jesus is calling you? Then come, I've been waiting for you!

Father, I come to Your outstretched hands, where I place the past. I lay within Your hands all those emotional encumbrances that have keep me in bondage to the past and stood in the way of Your best for me. I am ready to leave the past behind and strain forward to that which lies before me. In You, I can be set free from the past.

DAY 25

GIVE HIM YOUR BEST

"There came a woman having an alabaster box of ointment of spikenard very precious and she broke the box, and poured it on his head. And there were some that had <u>indignation</u> within themselves, and said, "why was this <u>waste</u> of the ointment made? For it might have been sold for more than three hundred pence, and have been given to the poor" (Mark 14:3-5 KJV).

Wasted! Nothing is wasted when you spend it on My Son, Jesus Christ. Your time is not wasted when you spend it with Him. Your money is not wasted when you use it for His purposes. Your gifts are not wasted when you use them for His glory. Your efforts are not wasted when you serve Him. You will encounter those who will be offended because you spend so much of your time working for My Kingdom and much of your finances to promote My Kingdom agenda. Do not focus on their sentiments. Set your eyes on the *prize,* for which I have called you in Jesus Christ (Philippians 3:14 NASB). Seek My Kingdom and put it first.

You are growing into perfection. You are spiritually maturing. You are putting first things first and that is a good thing, a heavenly thing. Never allow the feelings of others to cause you to misstep. Never allow the indignant actions or reactions of others to become the stimulus that causes you to stumble. You are to commit your life as a living sacrifice, holy, and acceptable unto Me. This IS your reasonable responsibility. I have instructed you "not to be conformed to this world [or the mindset of this world], but be transformed by the renewing of your mind" (Romans 12:2 NASB). By your obedience, you are doing the best and most acceptable thing for My Kingdom. You will be doing My perfect will (Romans 12:2 NKJV).

"If [I] be for [you], who can be against [you]" (Romans 8:31 KJV)? Let the naysayers live in their indignation. Do not allow them to put a wedge between you and Me. Be like the woman with the alabaster box. This woman was considered a sinner—an outcast. She had the *audacity* to enter (uninvited) into a Pharisee's house (of all people) and pass by all the surprised onlookers, in effort to enter into the presence of My Son, Jesus (her soon coming Savior). Once there, she knelt down humbly before Him and washed his feet with her tears, wiped them with the hairs of her head, and kissed and anointed them with the expensive contents of her renowned alabaster jar (Luke 7:36-38 NIV). She risked it all for the One who would die for her.

If it is your heart's desire to risk all for the One who died for you, why let the voices and actions of the *indignant* stand in the way? If you choose to give all your time, money, resources, and efforts to His Kingdom, have you not done only that which was your reasonable responsibility? Would you not consider it reasonable to give Him your best? The *indignant* did not die for you, My Son did. Come, worship at His feet today! Fall down before Him and wipe His feet with your grateful tears. Anoint Him with your love and tender care, for He has done it all for you. Come give Him your best. Come, worship your King. Come, I've been waiting for you!

Lord, I come to give myself to You, whereby I give You my heart, I give you my soul, I give You my life, and I give You everything that I own—I'll give You my best. I'll give my hands to serve You. I'll give my voice to proclaim You. I'll give my feet to walk in You. I'll give you my song to worship You. All that I am, and all that I have, I give to You.

DAY 26

HEAR MY VOICE

"And he said, go forth and stand upon the mount before the LORD. *And, behold, the* LORD *passed by, and a great and strong wind rent the mountains, and brake in pieces the rocks before the* LORD; *but the* LORD *was not in the wind: and after the wind an earthquake; but the* LORD *was not in the earthquake. And after the earthquake a fire; but the* LORD *was not in the fire: and after the fire a still small voice..."* (1 Kings 19:11-13 KJV).

While I chose to speak to My servant Elijah through a whisper, I can use any means and any form—wind, fire, earthquake...to speak. My ways of communicating vary with My purpose. To get Moses' attention, I spoke through a fiery bush. To get your attention, I may speak through your present circumstances.

When My Son cried out and gave up His spirit, the veil of "the temple was torn in two from top to bottom. The earth shook, the rocks split and the tombs broke open" (Matthew 27:50-52 NIV). I was *speaking* to all those who crucified Him and observed His death. When the people saw "all that was happening, they were terribly frightened and filled with awe" (Matthew 27:54 AMPC). What did they acknowledge? They acknowledged that Jesus Christ was truly My Son (Matthew 27:54). Did I not speak powerfully so that they could hear? I am still speaking through various means today. Do you not hear My distinct voice speaking to you?

"Indeed, [I] speak once or twice, yet no one notices it. In a dream, a vision of the night, when sound sleep falls on men, while they slumber in their beds, then [I] open the ears of men, and seal their instruction" (Job 33:14-16 NASB).

It is imperative that you train your spiritual ears to hear Me. It's My desire to share My heart and My thoughts with you. I spoke through My Word about the plans (plural) that I have for you. Scripture proclaims: "For I know the PLANS I have for you....PLANS to prosper you and not to harm you, PLANS to give you hope and a future" (Jeremiah 29:11 NIV). You see, I don't just have one plan for you in life. I have many plans that will come together from different directions and experiences to accomplish My purpose for your life. These plans that come from My mind and My heart—they are plans to PROSPER you. They are plans to give you blissful HOPE and a glorifying FUTURE.

You are living in a time such as this to accomplish My pre-ordained purposes for your life and My Kingdom. You are not alive today (by accident). You have been chosen. You are significant. Do you want to hear about My plans? Is it not worthwhile to incline your ear and wait to hear *My voice* speak of *My plans* for you? Tune into My frequency and I will speak. Come closer to Me and you will hear the sound of plans being shaped in My Kingdom for you. Come, I've been waiting for you!

Lord, I come near to hear You, where I'll incline my ear and listen for Your voice as You speak through Your Word, the mountains, the stars, earthquakes, or whatever wonders and ways that You choose to speak to me. Speak to me Lord and reveal Your heart to me. Speak Lord, I'm listening!

SECTION IV

THE GOODNESS OF GOD

Devotionals in this section speak to the heart of those who have accepted, embraced, and begun a love affair with Jesus Christ. You have come to know and trust God as your Father, your Healer, and your All in All. You have begun the journey of pruning and healing. You are now trusting and walking in the will of God. You are blooming and blossoming in God's grace and goodness. These devotionals will bring you peace, joy, and assuredness of the love God has for you. Rejoice, Rejoice, Rejoice, for God called you, and you answered His call!

DAY 27

O THE JOY OF HIS FAVOR

"A good man obtains favor from the Lord"
(Proverbs 12:2 NKJV).

I have openly declared that you are My own special treasure
(Deuteronomy 7:6 NLT). "I have called you by name; you
are Mine" (Isaiah 43:1 NKJV). I know you intimately and
personally. We have entered into sweet fellowship. When
you enter into relationship and fellowship with Me, you
receive certain benefits and privileges. Each day, I load you
with these heavenly benefits (Psalm 68:19 NKJV). These
benefits include: help and support; spiritual blessings and
prosperity; honor and rewards; grace and mercy... Because
you are "Mine," you have obtained favor in My sight and
acquired a favorable position in My Kingdom. It is a
"sweet" place to be. It is optimum living, when you are
living "inside" of My will and being the recipient of My
divine favor.

What price would you place on My "favor?" What "brick
and mortar" store can you go to purchase My "unmerited"
favor? You can't go buy it, and you can't earn it. It is
because of My goodness, and not yours, that you (the elect)
obtain this favor. In the world, when someone is favored
they are given preferential treatment. Likewise, I favor all
who have accepted My Son, Jesus Christ, as their Lord and
Savior. Once you have received Him as your Lord and

Savior, My royal Scepter will always be extended to you. As the ruling authority in My Kingdom, I have the power to crown you with favor, loving kindness and tender mercies (and so I have). "Because of [your] faith, Christ has brought you into this place of undeserved privilege, where [you] now stand, and [you] confidently and joyfully look forward to sharing [His] glory" (Romans 5:2 NLT). You are now a partaker of My blessings, grace and mercy. I have bestowed upon you My prosperity, which consists of: plenitude, freedom, security, wholeness, soundness, strength, breakthrough, well-being, joy, peace, contentment and so much more. There exist storehouses of blessings in My heavenly domain waiting to be poured out upon you.

Come, I want to load you with spiritual benefits! I want to give you a glimpse of what I have ordained for you. Come, I've been waiting for you!

Father, I come before Your throne of grace, where I praise and worship You for the wondrous favor You've shown me in life. My heart is filled with joy for all the fruits of Your grace that You've bestowed upon me.

DAY 28

IT IS FAITH THAT MOVES ME

"But without faith it is impossible to please him: for he that cometh to God must believe that He is, and that He is a rewarder of them that diligently seek Him"
(Hebrews 11:6 KJV).

In these difficult and challenging times, the faith of many are being severely stretched and tested. Global unrest is escalating. Nations are in distress. Morals have declined, and, in fact, being redefined. Relationships are strained and fractured. In the lives of many, the walls of *security* are broken down. "Men's hearts are failing them from fear and the expectation of those things which are coming on the earth" (Luke 21:26 NKJV). It is a time of great angst. But this is not the time to give in to hopelessness, for "when these things begin to come to pass, then look up, and lift up your [head], for your redemption draws near" (Luke 21:28 NKJV).

This is the time to exercise great faith in My Word and in My promises. You must strengthen your faith during these times. Without faith, it will be impossible to please Me (Hebrews 11:6 KJV). The enemy knows that faith is a vital part of our relationship. Therefore, your faith is that area that he will attack you the most. This is the time to have *Stephen-like* faith. A time to look up steadfastly into heaven,

91

regardless of the circumstances, and set your eyes on My glory (Acts 7:55 KJV). The enemy was defeated by Stephen's unwavering faith. You must be just as steadfast and resolute in the face of your own time of testing. Let it be a comfort to you that I will never abandon or forsake you in times of testing.

Faithful one, do not be shaken by the things you hear and see around you or in the world. Do not be distracted. This is a ploy of the enemy. Instead of being moved by his distractions, remain focused on My love and compassion during these troubling times. Be moved by My trustworthiness and My ability to protect and provide for you. Be moved by My ability to change any circumstance that you may face. Be moved by My goodness and My mercy.

While hell is breaking loose all around you, remember, I will keep in perfect peace those who place their trust in Me. Yes, if your thoughts are "*fixed*" on Me, I will "keep [you] in perfect peace" (Isaiah 26:3 NKJV). This means that you cannot take your eyes off of Me and put them on your problems. Have *Stephen-like* faith. As the vicious crowd stoned My servant, Stephen to death (for something he did not do), his faith moved Me. He wasn't looking at the angry crowd. He wasn't questioning My love for him. He wasn't trying to defend himself. He wasn't distracted by the circumstances surrounding him—no, his eyes were fixed upon My glory and it gave him hope and strength. He cried unto Me, the only one who could help him. He kneeled down and placed his fate in My hands and asked Me to forgive the ones who had slain him. I tell you, his faith moved Me!

Faithful one, your faith can move Me too. Regardless of

what is going on in your own life, or in the world around you, find ways to "move me" with your faith. Use each challenge as an opportunity to strengthen your faith and testimony. Use it as an opportunity to declare My goodness despite the circumstances that surround you. What a witness you will be for My Kingdom, when the world sees your steadfastness in the face of adversity. Are you in agreement? If so, then come, faithful one, enter into My rest. Shut the door on all your doubts and fears. Hide yourself in Me—your Refuge. Come, I've been waiting for you!

Father, I come seeking "Stephen-like" faith, whereby Your heart will be moved. I want unwavering faith that will keep my eyes fixed upon You, no matter the circumstance or the cost. I want faith that will challenge and silence all fear within me. I want faith that will move the mountains in my way. Lord, give me faith that moves You.

Acronym for F.A.I.T.H

FREELY
ABDICATE
IT
TO
HIM

DAY 29

THE POWER OF PRAYER

*"The heartfelt and persistent prayer of a righteous man (believer)
can accomplish much [when put into action and made effective by
God—It is dynamic and can have tremendous power]"*
(James 5:16 AMP).

Prayer has the power to move Me. This was demonstrated in the life of My faithful prophet Daniel. Daniel's prayers strengthen him to stand strong in faith, in the face of the adversity that surrounded him. His prayers enabled him to withstand the cultural and religious pressure and influence of his captors, without compromise. Daniel's prayers led to My special favor, provision, and blessing; and proved powerful enough to close the mouths of lions, when he faced the lions' den. Like Daniel, your prayers can move Me.

If you desire prayers that have the power to move Me, then your prayers have to be centered on Me. When the focus of your prayers are on you—your needs, your wants, and your problems, you walk away with the meager crumbs from My offering table instead of My fulfilling portion. Empowering prayer results when you let Me take center stage in your prayers and speak. When you covet and seek to hear that which is contained in My heart and in My mind, through prayer, I will share My plans, purposes, and direction for Your life, and impart bountiful spiritual blessings unto you.

Faith and obedience are keys to powerful prayer. If you

94

possess faith in My power, love, and faithfulness, and you walk in obedience to My will and My way, you have the power to move Me; and you can: "ask [according to My will] and it will be given to you; seek [especially that which is spiritual] and you will find; knock and the door [to My heart and provision] will be opened to you" (Luke 11:9 NIV).

Prayer has the power to move Me to act supernaturally in your heart and life. Fervent, unceasing, prayer empowers you to live the Christian life—for, I will work through your prayers. I will impart the knowledge of My will, precepts, and purposes. I will provide you with spiritual wisdom, insight, and discernment to guide your steps and walk in Me. I will increase your faith to *Stephen-like* faith that can move mountains in your life. I will strengthen you spiritually so that you can face and walk through life's trials and storms. I will work within your heart to develop a Christ-like character, a moral compass, and integrity that will enable you to walk in the manner I called you to live. I will equip you to serve Me and to bear spiritual fruit through the work you do unto Me (Colossians 1:9-11 AMP). I will give you a voice to proclaim Me. I will speak to that which afflicts and burdens you, and provide spiritual, emotional, and physical healing. I will place My spiritual armor around you to protect you from Satan's attacks, temptations, and landmines against your mind, body, and soul, in his attempt to corrupt your walk in Me. I will allow your story of *a walk in faith* to become a testimony for Me.

The power of prayer is immeasurable. It can save souls, change hearts, transform lives, strengthen the weary soul, grow faith, give sight to the spiritually blind, open the ears of the spiritually deaf, enable the crippled to walk in me, provide healing, calm raging storms in life, protect against the enemy, and move mountains.

Do you want the power to live the Christian life? If you do, come to Me in fervent, unceasing, prayer. I will answer and work in mighty ways. Come, sit at My feet, speak, and then be still, and I will share My heart and My mind with you. Come, I've been waiting for you.

God of wonders, I come to sit at Your feet, where I desire to hear You speak, display Your power, and work wonders through my prayers. Lord, I ask You to come, take center stage in my heart, my prayers, and my life.

DAY 30

GOD REMEMBERS

"For He remembered..."
(Psalm 105:42 KJV).

I remember when I created you in your mother's womb. You were a marvelous work. I will never forget your face, your voice, or anything else about you, for I have formed you from My very hands, and "I have inscribed you on the palms of My hands" (Isaiah 49:16 NKJV).

I remember My covenant with you: to "imprint my Laws upon your mind and upon your "innermost thoughts," and "engrave them" upon your heart [resulting in your rebirth in Me]; And that I will be your God and you will be reconciled to Me (Hebrews 8:10 AMPC). I recall how My covenant with you was executed. My Son [Jesus Christ], the Mediator, carried out the requirements of the covenant through His work at the Cross, and you performed your part through your faith in Him. Because of the fulfillment of My covenant, through your faith, you are forgiven, reconciled, and freed from sin's penalty; and I no longer remember your iniquity (Jeremiah 31:34 NKJV).

I remember My promises to you. I assured you that, If you seek Me in faith, I will provide salvation for your soul (Mark 16:16 NIV) and give you eternal life (John 10:28 NIV). More so, if you are walking in faith, I offer other promises to you. Amongst them: I will give you abundant life in Me (John 10:10 NASB); I will be with you wherever you go (Joshua 1:9

NIV); "I will never leave you nor forsake you" (Hebrews 13:5 ESV); I will provide a plan and a purpose for your life (Jeremiah 29:11 NIV); I will supply all of your needs (Philippians 4:19 NIV); I will strengthen you (Isaiah 40:29 NIV); I will hear your prayers (1 John 5:14 NIV); and I will not allow any difficulty [temptation or trial] to come into your life without purpose or which you will not be able to overcome (1 Corinthians 10:13 NIV).

I remember your faithfulness. I have watched every step you have taken in faith. When you have faced persecution, suffering, or rejection because of your faith in me, I have witnessed it. When you have walked through fiery trials, and have weathered life storms, with your eyes upon me, I saw it. When you have proclaimed Jesus Christ as your Savior and testified for Him, I have observed it. When you laid down your life and forsook what the world had to offer, to follow My will and My way, I recorded it in My heart. Your faithfulness has moved Me, and I will always remember it.

I remember your prayers. I recall each prayer that you have said unto Me. Each time you called out and inclined your ear to hear what was on My mind and contained within My heart, I spoke. When you sought provision and strength from Me, I readied My hands to work on your behalf. Times when you have cried out in brokenness and despair, I listened intently and provided comfort to your weary heart. When you uttered your need for Me, I came near and gave you all of Me.

I remember all your works of faith and labor of love for Me (1 Thessalonians 1:3 ESV). You have proven your faith in Me through all the work you have done for Me (James: 2:20 NKJV). I've watched as you have worked to awaken souls to Me and touched hearts and lives for Me. Know that Your efforts to further My kingdom message and purpose have not gone unnoticed, for I have treasured and contained each and every one in My heart and memory.

Now that I have opened My heart and revealed some of my remembrances concerning you, come near to Me and share what you recall about Me. I want to hear. Come, I've been waiting for you.

Father, I come before Your altar of remembrance, where I reflect upon your faithfulness in my life. Knowing that I am remembered by You in so many ways, and that You have inscribed me on the palms of Your hands, invokes emotions within me that I cannot describe in words. I can say that You are an amazing God and that I will always remember the day that You called Me to Yourself and delivered My soul.

DAY 31

THE GOODNESS OF GOD

"For the Lord is good; His mercy and lovingkindness are everlasting, His faithfulness [endures] to all generations" *(Psalm 100:5 AMP).*

My goodness is defined in all that I am, and is displayed through all that I do—for I am forever faithful, just, loving, kind, merciful, and compassionate. In My goodness, I provide, protect, strengthen, heal, empower, and shepherd. Accounts of My goodness speak through scripture and move hearts.

The ultimate expression of My goodness is My unfailing love which was demonstrated at the *Cross,* where I provided Jesus Christ, as the Sacrificial Lamb, who took your place, bore your sins upon Himself, withstood the *Cross,* and died to give you life in Me.

My goodness is demonstrated in My plans for your life— "plans to prosper you... plans to give you hope and a future" (Jeremiah 29:11 NIV). This plan includes your salvation which was fulfilled through the Cross. This plan delivered your soul from everlasting separation from Me. Still, I have other plans for your life. In My goodness, I have provided for you to have a resurrected life, where you can walk in newness, restoration, forgiveness, and transformation. I have prepared for you to lead a purpose-driven life, whereby you can faithfully live out and fulfill My ordained purpose for your life. You will become an extension of My hands, heart, eyes, ears, and voice to this world that is crying out for a Savior. I have also planned for you to possess and live the Spirit-filled life, whereby you surrender to the Holy Spirit, giving Him access to every part of your heart and life, enabling Him to live and work through you to produce spiritual fruit, grow your faith, equip and empower you to be fruitful in your work for Me, and transform you into a powerful witness for Me.

My goodness is reflected in the spiritual gifts and provisions that I impart unto you. I have given you the most powerful and wondrous spiritual gift—the Holy Spirit. He dwells within you to guide you into all truth, wisdom and spiritual discernment. He enables you to walk uprightly in Me and equips you with the spiritual gifts to serve and glorify Me. In My goodness, I have provided spiritual healing for damaged emotions and other spiritual afflictions. I also gird you in spiritual armor to guard you against the enemy's landmines.

My Goodness will continue into eternity. Awaiting you are heavenly crowns to bestow upon you for your faithful walk in Me. My outstretched hands await to give [according to works of faith]: the crown of beauty [instead of ashes] (Isaiah 61:3 NIV), the crown of righteousness (2 Timothy 4:8 NIV), the crown of life (James 1:12 NIV), the crown of victory [incorruptible crown] (1 Corinthians 15:54-57 NKJV), the crown of glory (1 Peter 5:1-4 NKJV), and the crown of rejoicing (1 Thessalonians 2:19 NKJV). Know, as the God of Wonders, I will show you amazing wonders upon your triumphant entry into My heavenly Kingdom.

As you walk along life's journey, you'll see signposts reflecting My goodness along the path. At the end of the road of life, you'll experience the outpouring of My goodness as I welcome you into My waiting arms. Come, I've been waiting for you!

Father, I come to You with a song in my heart. My heart sings of the goodness You have shown me through Your unfailing love, faithfulness, and provision. Each day I awaken to Your goodness and it follows me all day long. At night, Your goodness watches over me. There is no place that I can go, nor any season that I face in life, where Your goodness is not found. Lord, You are so good to me.

Scripture References

Lamb of God: John 1:29 NKJV; Philippians 2:10 KJV; Isaiah 1:18 KJV; Psalm 34:8 KJV; Revelation 21:27 KJV; John 1:16 NASB; Revelation 22:17 AMP

I Have Come to Set You Free: Matthew 27:3-4 NLT; 1 Peter 5:8 KJV; Luke 22:31 KJV; John 10:10 KJV; Isaiah 53:10 AMP; Psalm139: 13-16 AMP; Ephesians 1:6-7 NKJV; Ephesians 2:7 KJV

My Declarations of Love for You: Jeremiah 31:3 TM; Song of Solomon 7:10 NLT; John 3:16 NLT; Hebrews 12:2 NLT; Romans 5:8 NIV; Psalm 56:8 KJV; Luke 7:37-38 KJV; Matthew 10:30 KJV; Zechariah 2:8 KJV; Hosea 2:23 AMP; 1 John 1:9 AMP; Romans 8:35, 38-39 NLT; Isaiah 54:10 ESV

There Is No Other God: Isaiah 45:5 KJV; Exodus 3:14 KJV; Psalm 131:1 KJV; Isaiah 44:6 KJV; John 1:3 KJV; Genesis 1:3 KJV; Ezekiel 28:15 NKJV; Philippians 2:8-11 KJV Hebrews 4:15 KJV; Psalm 103:12 NLT; Exodus 31:13 KJV; Psalm 23:1 KJV; Psalm 46:1 KJV; Exodus 15:26 KJV; Philippians 4:19 KJV; Jeremiah 23:6 KJV; Judges 6:24 KJV; Hebrews 13:5 NKJV

Drink From the Fountain of My Salvation: Isaiah 12:1-3 NLT; Amos: 8:11 KJV; Jeremiah 2:13 KJV; Jeremiah 2:11 NIV; Ecclesiastes 1:2 KJV; Psalm 63:1 NKJV; Revelation 22:17 NASB; Isaiah 51:3 NIV

Come Follow Me: Matthew 16:24 KJV; Mark 8:38 NKJV; Deuteronomy 6:5 NASB; Matthew 4:19 KJV.

A Faithful Priest: 1 Samuel 2:35 NASB; Hebrews 7:26 NASB; Ephesians 2:20-22 NASB; Luke 17:33 NLT; Luke 11:42 KJV; 1 Peter 2:9 ESV

Why Are You Downcast O My Soul: Psalm 43:5 KJV; Romans 8:1 NLT; Psalm 107: 10 NLT; Luke 4:18 KJV; John 13:34 NIV;

Matthew 6:12 KJV

Broken Vessels: Psalm 31:12 AMPC; Luke 7:37-38 NIV; Luke 9:16 KJV; Ezekiel 47:12 NIV; Acts 26:14 KJV; Jeremiah 18:4 KJV; 2 Timothy 2:20 TM

The Storms of Life: Psalm 107:28-30 AMPC; John 8:32 KJV; John 16:33 KJV; Acts 28:3,11 KJV; 2 Corinthians 11:22-33 NLT; Nahum 1:5 NIV; Psalm 13:1 NASB; Psalm 107:31-33 KJV

Fear Not: Isaiah 41: 10 KJV; Joshua 1:9 KJV; 1 Peter 5:7 NIV; Psalm 138:8 NKJV; Philippians 4:6-7 ESV; Numbers 23:19 NKJV; Romans 8:28 KJV; 2 Timothy 1:7 KJV; Hebrews 4:10 KJV

Lifter of My Head: Psalm 3:3 KJV; 1 Peter 1:6-7 NLT; Revelation 2:17, 26, 3:5 NLT; 2 Corinthians 4:18 NLT; Psalm 40:2-3,11 NLT; Psalm 121 NKJV; Isaiah 45:2 & ASV; NKJV; 2 Timothy 2:1 KJV;

My Love Never Fails: 1 Corinthians 13:8 NIV; Ephesians 3:18 NIV; Isaiah 49:16 NKJV

Let My Will Be Done: Luke 22:42 KJV; Isaiah 55:8-9 NKJV; Matthew 20:22 KJV; Matthew 16:25 KJV; Matthew 26:39 KJV; Romans 8:7 AMP; Ephesians 5:27 NLT; Luke 14:28 NLT; Matthew 6:10 NLT

You Say You Cannot Hear Me: John 10:27 NKJV

Hem of His Garment: Luke 8:43-48 NKJV; John 1:14 KJV; Psalm 107:20 KJV

Establishing A Testimony: Psalm 78:5 KJV; Revelation 12:11 KJV;

Controlled by My Spirit: Galatians 5:25 AMPC; Matthew 7:17 KJV; Galatians 5:16 HCSB; John 14:26 NIV; Romans 12:2 AMP; John 10:7 KJV.

Where Have You Come From And Where Are You Going?:

Genesis 16:8 NKJV; John 18:15-27 & 21:15-17 NKJV; 1 Kings 19:1-3 NJKV; Job 10:1-22 ESV; Jonah 1 ESV

Will You Be The One? 2 Corinthians 5:20 HCSB; 1 John 2:15 KJV; Mark 8:36 KJV; Matthew 28:18-20 KJV

Be Ye Holy: 1 Peter 1:16 KJV; 1 Peter 2:16 AMPC; Psalm 119: 160 KJV; John 12:48 NKJV; 1 Peter 1:16 NKJV; Joshua 24:15; 2 Timothy 3:2-5 NKJV; 1 Peter 2:11-12 KJV; 2 Corinthians 7:1 NIV; 2 Corinthians 10:5 NASB

Put Me First: 1 Kings 17:13 NIV/AMP; 1 Kings 17:13-14 AMPC

Seek My Counsel: Psalm 33:11 NASB; Psalm 32:8 NASB

Leave The Past Behind: Philippians 3:13-14 AMPC; Genesis 50:20 KJV; 2 Corinthians 5:17 TM; 1 John 1:9 NIV; Matthew 6:14-15 NASB; Ezekiel 36:26-28 TM

Give Him Your Best: Mark 14: 3-5 KJV; Philippians 3:14 NASB; Romans 12:2 NASB; Romans 8:31 KJV; Luke 7:36-38 NIV

Hear My Voice: 1 Kings 19:11-13 KJV; Matthew 27:50-52 NIV; Matthew 27:54 AMPC; Job 33:14-16 NASB; Jeremiah 29:11 NIV

O The Joy of His Favor: Proverbs 12:2 NKJV; Deuteronomy 7:6 NLT; Isaiah 43:1 NKJV; Psalm 68:19 NKJV; Romans 5:2 NLT

It is Faith That Moves Me: Hebrews 11:6 KJV; Luke 21:26, 28 NKJV; Acts 7:55 KJV; Isaiah 26:3 NKJV

The Power of Prayer: James 5:16 AMP; Luke 11:9 NIV; Colossians 1:9-11 AMP

God Remembers: Psalm 105:42 KJV; Isaiah 49:6 NKJV; Hebrews 8:10 AMPC; Jeremiah 31:34 NKJV; Mark 16:16 NIV; John 10:28 NIV; John 10:28 NASB; Joshua 1:9 NIV; Hebrews 13:5 ESV; Jeremiah 29:11 NIV; Philippians 4:19 NIV; Isaiah 40:29 NIV; 1

John 5:14 NIV; 1 Corinthians 10:13 NIV; 1 Thessalonians 1:3 ESV; James 2:20 NKJV.

The Goodness of God: Psalm 100:5 AMP; Jeremiah 29:11 NIV; Isaiah 61:3 NIV; 2 Timothy 4:8 NIV; James 1:2 NIV; 1 Corinthians 9:25;   15:54-57 NKJV; 1 Peter 5:1-4; 1 Thessalonians 2:19 NKJV

ABOUT THE AUTHOR

Barbara's life is a reflection of the redemptive power of God's love and forgiveness. Through the heartfelt messages presented in this book, God has bestowed upon her the gift of communicating what He has shown and shared with her along her spiritual journey. The desire of Barbara's heart is to be used for God's divine will and purpose. For the past nine years, Barbara has been part of the TCT Television Ministry Network. Barbara resides in Greensboro, North Carolina, where she faithfully serves God in her community. She has one daughter, Raquele Brimmage and one granddaughter, Destiny Brimmage.

If you would like to contact Barbara to let her know how this devotional has impacted your life, you have the following options:

scribalexpressions17@gmail.com
www.scribalexpressions.blog

You may also leave a review of this book on Amazon.

NOTES

NOTES

Christian Life/Devotional
ISBN 978-0-9986554-0-6

110

45083264R00068

Made in the USA
Middletown, DE
24 June 2017